A B-Girl in a B-Boy World

My Auto Biography

Kim-A-Kazi

"A B-Girl in a B-Boy World - From the Streets of Brooklyn to Breakdancing Stardom," by Kim (Kim-A-Kazi) Valente. ISBN 978-1-62137-747-4.

Published by Virtualbookworm.com Publishing, P.O. Box 9949, College Station, TX, 77842.

Original artwork by Peteski

Dedications

I dedicate this book to my wonderful husband, Louis Valente, and my loving son, David Perelez, for they are my support team. For all the times you had to tip-toe around the house so I could write in peace, I thank you.

To my mother, Monica, who has always given me her support and always told me I have the talent to become a writer, I thank you for always being honest and believing in me. Thank you, Mom.

I dedicate this book to my sister, Doll JaeCie—you will always be in my heart; I wouldn't trade the times we shared for anything. To my friend, Darlene Lewis, who set my feet upon this path, I will always be grateful to you. To all of my fellow B-Boys and B-Girls in Greece, especially my Sista B-Girl Veester Valentin, along with Giorgos & B-Boy Loyal T, I can always feel your love no matter how many miles are between us. To Manu, another friend whose love and support far surpass the great distance between us, I cherish you and I thank you for your feedback.

A special thanks to Jerri Council and Shake, who are family to me and who have been there from the beginning, I am proud of how brightly your own stars are shining. Always supporting me and giving me unconditional love, as well as my "Sista" and honorary "Doll" Samantha Allende, who always has my back and my heart. Incredible Breakers who are my "Brothas," we shared such great times in the beginning of our careers. To TG and Keith Rodgers, aka Bon Rock, for your respect and support. Nick Abreu, always a source of love and encouragement.

There are so many names I could include, people I have never even laid eyes on who have shown me such love and support and who appreciate all of my hard work and contributions to Hip Hop. I appreciate your support.

Mostly I dedicate this book to all the real dancers out there, the ones who do not do it for fame, but because they'd rather stop breathing than stop dancing. It is that kind of passion that bonds all true dancers.

Note to Readers:

While writing this book, I was torn. I did not want this book to be perceived as "negative" or as if I "was purposely hating on anyone". At the same time, I felt I cannot leave out certain facts. I have to tell the story the way it happened, even though it may not shine a positive light on certain people. The bottom line is; these events did happen. I can no more change the past as it happened than I can be responsible for other people's actions and behavior. All I can do is tell you how it happened, plain and simple.

In the same respect, I will always give credit where credit is due, regardless of my own personal feelings. This is something that many people out there will not do. If they do not like you, they will never say anything good about you. When you tell a story and you speak of history, you need to be as accurate as you possibly can. I myself have double checked my own memories with those who were there with me to ensure that my memories were accurate.

No one has the right to rewrite history, especially to suit their own personal preferences. If you ask me, it's not just wrong, it's criminal. This is what has been going on for decades and it needs to stop. I would think people would be furious to find out that they have been lied to, especially by those they look up to. I find many people are too scared to speak up or out against many of these people. What is worse are those who were present back in the day and who know what is being said are all lies, but stay silent. Shame on them.

So I have decided to tell the truth without prejudice or malice because it was what occurred, and if I am going to take you on this journey with me, I want you all to have the full experience. The joy, laughter, the struggles and the obstacles that we faced. And as with all things, the jealousy and the injustice that many of us dealt with back then, and today as well. I hope you enjoy my story and I wish you all lots of success on your own journeys. There is nothing you can't do if you give it your all.

Love, Peace and Blessings,

Kim-A Kazi

Stop the Presses!

Just before this book went to print, a funny thing happened. Finally, after 30 long years, I got to speak to my friend, Mr. Robert Taylor (better known to most as "Lee" from the 1984 Hip-Hop movie, "Beat Street" Robert also appeared with The Dynamic Dolls in the video, "The Beat Street Strut." Robert is such a gracious and humble man and here is what he wanted to add to the book:

I would like to say that Kim is a special part of the Hip-Hop culture and is an incredible B-girl with charisma, style and fitness. Kim is one of the first B-girls who started breaking and opened the doors for all the B-girls today. She is such an inspiring person who fought all the odds of becoming a B-girl and became one of the pioneers in Hip-Hop today. Kim, I salute you for your contribution to the culture known today around the world as Hip-Hop. We Owe You.

Robert Taylor – aka "Lee"

Introduction

Imagine yourself standing on a stage in front of fifty thousand fans, and they are all screaming and applauding for you! It is one heck of a feeling, but I never took it as "Oh look at me, they love me, I am amazing". I always felt like "All right, I did my job, I did my best and they are showing me their approval". Either way it was a great feeling.

Most of the time I don't think the audience knew what to make of me, especially when I performed with just the guys. Here was this female, a white female, and although I looked the part and I performed the routine flawlessly with the guys (The Dynamic Breakers), when I stepped forward to perform my solo it was like the audience was almost silent, holding their breath. I suspect many of them were prepared to laugh me off stage or boo and hiss, but as soon as I started popping, the audience would explode with applause. There was no better expression of acceptance to me, and it meant just as much to me each and every time it happened.

What made it even better was when I looked to my left and my right; my crew members were standing next to me. We were more than just friends—we were family. I think it is interesting how we all came back together again to form The Dynamic Breakers, and later The Dynamic Dolls, after working together years earlier. No matter which Dynamic Crew, The Dynamic Rockers, The Dynamic Breakers or The Dynamic Dolls, each crew is a huge part of creating the dance sector of Hip Hop and are a large part of Hip Hop history. In this book, you will realize many of the reasons why.

I am not comfortable referring to myself as a "legend" or an "icon," but you see, I do not. I did not give myself these titles. They were bestowed upon me by my peers and fans. There are many people who refer to themselves as "legends," but it is not a title one can give to oneself. *Just because you were around back then, does not mean you warrant such an honor.* When you can do something amazing and do it better than anyone else, or if you were the first to do or bring something into the world, then maybe you deserve such a title—but it still has to be given to you. Which is probably why I see many of the B-Boys from my days trying to take credit for being the first to do this, or the first to do that. Tsk, tsk,

Now as you turn these pages, you will learn some real Hip Hop history, and hear some cool and funny stories, which are accompanied by photographs from my own photo album. So come join me as I take you through my journey of being...

"A B-Girl in a B-Boy World"

Table of Contents

Chapter 1 —The Beginning

From the time I was born, it was apparent that I was going to be a very active child. My mother said I practically came out dancing.

The first time my parents brought me home, they put me down to sleep in my crib. My mother came back in a short time later to check on me and I was now on my back. My mother knew she had put me to sleep on my stomach, but because it is unheard of that a 10-day-old infant could turn over, she assumed she was mistaken. My mother put me back on my stomach and left the room. Again, she came back in to find me on my back. My mother began to believe she was going crazy, but eventually she witnessed my amazing feat for herself, and then with other family members. Definitely a sign of things to come!

Dancing was always a part of my life. I can remember being about three years old at a birthday party. They were having a dance contest for the kids, so naturally I joined in. I can remember several adults were standing next to me, and I heard them talking about me.

They were amazed that such a little kid could know such modern adult dance moves and execute them perfectly. I seem to remember even back then that I had a gift when it came to dancing, just by the way people reacted to me.

When I was nine years old, I went with my mom and my aunt to pick up my cousin from her tap dance class. We arrived early, and I watched intently as the class tapped away to the song "Frosty the Snowman" for the winter recital. There was a bin with extra tap shoes in it, I found a pair that fit me and I followed along with the class from behind the viewing glass. In just a few minutes, I had learned the entire tap routine. After class, all of the children took turns being measured for their costumes that they

1

would be wearing for the recital. While they were doing that, I went into the classroom.

What a magical place, I thought. Just being in that studio made me feel alive. With most of the studio to ourselves, my cousin and I started playing around, and we were doing the tap routine. The dance teacher was both puzzled and amazed. Where did this child come from? She could not believe that I had learned the same routine it took the class weeks, even months to learn, in just minutes. Not to mention I had never taken a tap lesson in my life. Heck, I never even wore a pair of tap shoes before that day. As you can see from the photo, I was put in the class and performed front and center at the dance recital.

My love for dancing continued throughout my life. My sister Kristine, who is one year older than me, along with our cousin would raid my mother's closet and pick out our costumes. Then we would pick a song to perform to, and I would choreograph a routine. I find it amazing that I was a natural choreographer from early childhood. I did not know I was doing anything special—it was just a natural thing for me to do. Once we had our song, our wardrobe and our routine, we would gather anyone who was available to watch (which usually consisted of my mom and my two aunts). Sometimes we would spring into action whenever company came over. What a bunch of hams we were!

As teenagers, we recruited our friends to join in our performances, and they were happy to do so. We would have hours of fun, and eventually we had a pretty good show with an array of talent. Until this day, my brothers and I still laugh about an improv routine I put together to the song "Walking in a Winter Wonderland." I had made us props for that performance, I used the cardboard tubes from rolls of wrapping paper. and I wrapped red ribbon around them to make candy cane walking sticks. Hey, you had to be creative back then—remember, there were no video game systems (until Atari came out), How primitive.

What I also find funny is that I used to make up games all of the time for me and my brothers to play when we were bored. I made up a name for one of the games—it was called

"Boogaloo." Now, keep in mind I was about ten or eleven years old and never heard the word. Just another ironic coincidence.

I never seemed to sit still. In the middle of a baseball game or a game of skelly when it wasn't my turn, I would be doing handstands or some other form of gymnastics I had taught myself. The street was my gymnasium, and I became pretty good at gymnastics. I remember making up this one move, where I would sit on the ground and go right into a back walkover. It was a great move. During the next Summer Olympics, I learned that move was called a "Valdez" and I had not invented it. However, I'd never seen it before.

One night when I was around twelve or thirteen, I was at this teen disco—you know, no alcohol, just for kids—and my friends had entered me in the dance contest they were having. When I saw who the next contestant was, I sat down against the wall and deemed myself out of the contest. It was the owner's niece. She was not better than me, not by a long shot. She did about four different steps and just repeated them until the song ended. I knew it was fixed, and I was not accustomed to losing dance contests—especially to the likes of her.

The DJ called my name and I was still sitting on the floor against the wall, in the same position I told you about earlier. My friends grabbed my extended left leg, dragged me onto the dance floor and left me sitting in the center of it. Oh well, now I had no choice. When the music began I was sitting on the floor, so I went straight into a "Valdez," the back walkover I just told you about. So I was now on my feet, and off I went. I gave them all of my best moves and tricks, even though I knew Miss Four Steps would win. The crowd went wild, and afterward the people told me they thought the whole thing was part of my act—you know, when my friends dragged me onto the dance floor.

Even though I had no chance of winning first place (I took second that night), I still gave it everything I had. After that night it was clear that the dance contest was fixed, and a lot of people complained. They cut the dance contests out for a while.

That was the only dance contest I ever lost. I entered a few with The Dolls, but I will get to that a little later.

Even in my grade school, someone would bring a small radio to school and at lunch time we would make a circle and dance after lunch in the cafeteria. At that time we were doing dances like The Bump, The Hustle, and some other dances—I do not know if they had names. I always hung out with all kinds of people, and we lived in a mixed neighborhood so everyone would bring a little something different to the dance party.

Ah, Kenilworth Place down by the Junction; Flatbush Ave in Brooklyn, New York—the best block ever. We always had something going on there. Stoopball, punch ball, stickball, baseball, and football, hockey, basketball, tag, skelly, Johnny on a pony, hot peas and butter, Statue, and a few games I made up.

We would ride our skateboards and jump garbage cans we'd lined up. Only the bravest and the best would be left in the game after three, four, five and even six garbage cans. We would even jump cars, too.

What does any of this have to do with dancing? A lot! I always had so much energy, and I had a lot of power too. I was always strong. I would push the envelope to see what else I could do. For example, when I taught myself how to do a handstand, I mastered it until I could stay in a handstand for as long as I wanted. But then once I accomplished that, I had to see what else I could do, which led to a one-arm handstand, and walking on my hands. Then I had to see if I could walk up and down steps and so on. But here is the funny thing—I remember after doing the one-arm handstand, I would do a half-twist (a 180 if you will) before landing on my feet. Then I moved on to a full turn on my hand. (Beginning to sound familiar?)

Now I am **not** saying I invented 1990s (or 2001s), because I didn't. However there are several break dance moves that I was doing without even knowing what I was doing at the time. I did the same thing with headstands. During a gymnastics show at school I did what I can only describe as quarter head spins. I went into a headstand and I turned to the west, then the south, east and north. And I also used to do floats, except with all of these moves, it never occurred to me to spin. I see all of these things as stepping stones to what would come to be later in my life.

I never took gymnastics, but I figured if I could learn how to do a few back flips and those tumble-saults they did in the air with no hands, I would come close to flying, I had the strength and the guts—I just did not know how to use them. I wanted to go, go, go; take off and fly through the air.

This boy who lived around the corner from me had a dad who worked in the YMCA down the block. This boy had a crush on me (although I do not know how any of those boys liked me at that age; I was just like a boy myself). Anyway, Joseph snuck me into the YWCA and let me watch the girls do gymnastics. I was so envious of those girls.

Somehow I had worked my way into the class. I had my first experience on the uneven bars, the balance beam, and the horse. I got away with it for a little while, sneaking in and joining the class, until one day I was busted. The teachers were so impressed with me, amazed that I had never taken a class. They said I was extremely talented and they wanted to train me. They sent me home with the forms for my mother to sign so I could join. My mother could not afford to send me for gymnastic lessons. I returned the forms and told them the bad news.

They would not accept no for an answer, so they actually went to my house and spoke—no, actually begged my mother to let me join. They even offered to cut the fee in half, but no dice. I know this may sound funny to you but, I know I could have made the Olympics in gymnastics. I had such power and flexibility, and the drive. It seemed all I had to do was envision something, and then pretend I knew how to do it.

I did the same thing with ice skating. The very first time I had ever gone ice skating, I learned how to go backwards and I learned how to spin and do an arabesque. I always wanted to be a gymnast, but it was not to be. (The spin I did on the ice comes into play later in the story.) So, I would have to find another way to "fly."

Me (R). 9 yrs old- Tap dance recital to "Frosty the Snowman"

My sister Kristine (L), me (M) and a cousin (R) dressed in my mother's accessories, ready to perform a routine I choreographed while lip-syncing. Check out those platform shoes!

As my sister's interests changed, I performed more with my brothers. If you were a kid in the 1970s you may remember a show called "Shields and Yarnell." They were a married couple who became famous for their robotic skits (you can see their performances on youtube.com).

That was my next project. I would teach my brother how to do the robot (funny, another peek into my future) and we would do skits just like Shields and Yarnell. I made

7

that reference because when I got into Hip Hop, I actually began "popping" before break dancing. I think it is ironic how the talents I nurtured early on in my childhood came into play later when I started break dancing. Moves such as the robot, gymnastics, pre-break dance moves, and especially choreography.

Now as a young teenager I began going to the dance clubs, mostly in Brooklyn (known as discotheques back in the day). At first I went to the teeny-bopper clubs such as Patches and Pinocchio's, which did not serve alcohol. Not long after that, I hit the adult clubs such as Scandals, Lamours, Penrods, and a host of other clubs. I did not drink alcohol. I was interested in dancing and guys.

I had always heard about this big club in Manhattan called The Fun House. I had no interest in going there for several reasons; one of which was it was strictly a gay club. Later it turned into a regular club and my mom worked there bartending, and my Uncle Monk was an owner of The Fun House—so I guess that was why I was able to get in, even though I was under age.

The Fun House alone should be inducted into the Hip Hop Hall of Fame, because that place was a breeding ground for many major stars, including Madonna herself. To many who were there, it is common knowledge that many of Madonna's earlier dance moves, and even her style of dressing, came from the dancers at the Fun House. Even in her movie "Desperately Seeking Susan," she is in the bathroom and uses the hand dryer to dry her hair and underarms. This was a regular thing we ladies did in the bathroom at the Fun House. Some brought their own blow dryers and others used the hand dryer, turning the nozzle upside down to dry off or dry their hair after washing it in the sinks. So it is safe to say that The Fun House had a great deal of influence on Madonna as well.

Madonna was a regular there, and I would see her all the time. We had a few brief conversations in the VIP room, but she was—let's say incoherent, most of the time. You never knew who you were going to run into at The Fun House or in the VIP room.

I was sitting in the VIP room one night (the VIP room was connected to the DJ booth) and who comes walking out of the DJ booth? Herbie Hancock. He was carrying one of his albums, and for some reason he just gave it to me! I still have it today. I carried that album all night long and all the way home.

The house deejay for The Fun House was Jellyboan, AKA John "Jellybean" Benitez. He would rock the house from his DJ booth, which was inside a giant clown's mouth. Jellybean dated Madonna, and they worked on many of her songs together. Jellybean still works in the music world. For more information on Jellybean, you can Google him or look him up on youtube.com.

The Fun House always had a star-packed weekend. They did not only have amazing talent on one night; they would have great talent there Friday night, and then another group or singer Saturday night, I have my date book in my hand as I write this: on March 26th, a Friday night, they had Grace Jones (what a crazy freak show that was) and Saturday night they had Stone singing "Time." As I look through this book, it is amazing how many legends performed at The Fun House: Soul Sonic Force, Jimmy Spicer, Jimmy Castor, Run DMC, New Edition—I could go on and on.

The Fun House was where I met many people who would become important in my life, in one way or another. Many of them would become my crew members in one break dance crew or another. Even today I am very good friend with Nick Abreu, who was another permanent fixture at The Fun House. Nick was one of those people who could float from one end of The Fun House to the other and fit right in.

Hip Hop dancers had the back stage, the "Buggers" and Kick Dancers were by the center stage. Then you had your Loft dancers and all others on the main dance floor, and in many other areas throughout the club. It was a buffet of dance styles. The only place where you did not go to dance was upstairs. Upstairs is where people went when they wanted to do things in private, like drugs or fooling around.

Other than the game room, where people went to play video games and get something to eat or drink.

There were so many nooks and crannies at The Fun House, it was easy to get lost by choice or by accident. My friend Nick I was just telling you about was telling me about his first experience at The Fun House (everyone has a first time story). Nick said that a friend told him he was being taken to a club where all of the best dancers go. Nick figured he was going to walk in and show these people what he could do, "Man was I wrong," Nick laughed.

He could not believe his eyes when he got passed the Fun House mirrors at the entrance, "This incredible energy hits you, and you know you have just walked into some place different than anywhere else you have ever been to." Nick said he was amazed at all of the different styles of dance going on under one roof, but what really got him was just how great these dancers were. He always tells me, "I will never forget going to the back of the club and seeing you and Dynamic going off." He was shocked to see Breakers doing choreography, and when he saw a female spinning guys, he could not believe it.

Nick told me he said, "Well if she can do that, so can we," and that is when he and his crew began incorporating break dancing into their dance styles. We do a lot of reminiscing together. We both find funny to think we were friends way back then, and here we are decades later, reconnected.

Who would have thought back then we would be discussing our great times at The Fun House almost forty years later? Nick is one guy who has no problem giving props to other dancers, and he has been working on a very important documentary about The Fun House. It is a major part of so many people's history, and a large part of Hip Hop history as well. We look forward to its debut.

Our territory–The Backstage at The Fun House, where break dancing ruled!

"The Juice Crew" from top left- Kim-A-Kazi, Idalis De Leon, Lizette & Melissa

Below, me in the crowd; this is on the cover of a CD

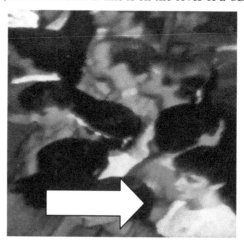

Also taken @ The Fun House like previous page.

Spinner (Dynamic Rockers) in Webbo pants / At The Roxy after the contest

Below, the famous DJ booth at The Fun House where Jellybean worked his magic.

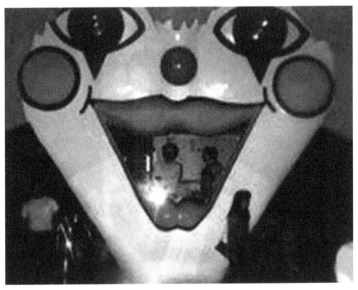

Chapter 2 – It's Just Begun

I can honestly say that so much history started at The Fun House.

Before break dancing hit the clubs, we were all doing a style of dance called "The Webbo." We wore these very baggy pants, a crop top tee shirt, and ankle suede boots; I had them in every color. If you have seen either of the two "Breakin" movies, then you have seen this style of clothing on Shrimp and Shabba-doo in those movies, as well as in the previous photos.

I had made many friends through dance, and we formed a dance crew which was later given the name "The Juice Crew" by Jellybean himself. There were approximately sixteen of us, which kept increasing, and we all shared a passion for dancing. However, the group started with seven dancers. Tony "White Lightning," Idalis, Lizette, Gary, Mickey, Jose, and myself. The Incredible Breakers and the rest joined us later.

As in all dance crews, we all had nicknames. Mine was Spinner. One night I was wearing my Juice Crew shirt with my name "Spinner" on the back and some guy called me over. He was sitting on the back stage and he said to me, "Hey, that's my name," pointing to my shirt. He told me we would have to battle for the name. Then he asked me, "Why do they call you Spinner?" So I showed him. He was like, "The name is yours." But it wasn't mine for long, and Elio is still known as "Spinner" to date.

Out of all of the amazing things I had learned to do, *this spin* is the top move I wish I had on film. The best way to describe it is, when you watch ice skating and a skater does that really fast, continuous spin that looks like a tornado and goes faster and faster as they pull their arms in close to their body; well, that is what I used to do. Except I did it on the floor and without ice skates. It really was amazing, even if I do say so myself. And I have never seen *another human being* do the same spin. Oh, I have seen dancers do some really nice, long spins, but nothing comes close to the one I did.

I thank goodness that I have witnesses who can testify to this spin (the only one done in this book). It was a matter of balance and finding your core. And practice, of course—lots of practice. But once you find that "sweet spot" with any move, it is easy.

I really wish I could still do that spin. Not only was it really something to see, but it was a lot of fun to do, too.

The start of my famous spin that won me the name Spinner.

Both photos taken at The Fun House

Us! On the cover of The Village Voice newspaper. I'm by the guy's foot on the right. My face is above his heel.

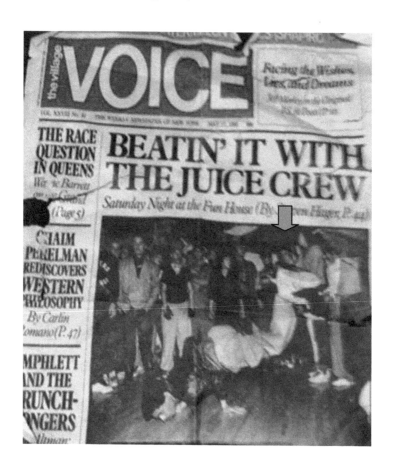

One of my earlier crazy "Fun House "outfits—this was pre-Hip Hop

Below: It's very hard to see, but just below the balloons is Grace Jones performing at The Fun House. That was a wild show, for sure!

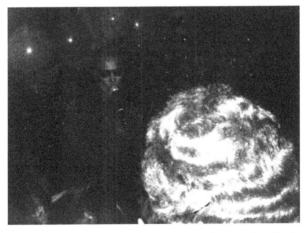

You would think that dancing continuously all through the night and into to the next morning would be enough, even for the most hyperactive person. But no, not for us. We would leave The Fun House when it closed somewhere around 6 a.m. Sometimes earlier, sometimes later—it changed from weekend to weekend, especially if the place got raided, which really sucked. The entire place would pile

17

out into the street and try to decide where to go next. Home was never an option.

Do you want to hear how sick we were? We would bring a change of clothes, sometimes even more than one change of clothes; along with deodorant and a washcloth so we could clean up in the bathroom. Some people got carried away and brought body wash, a hair dryer, a toothbrush and toothpaste—everything but the bathroom sink, because they had those there already! After the club closed, we would all walk over to our favorite breakfast shop and have a little nourishment before we headed over to Washington Square Park.

Washington Square Park became our daytime dance club, where we would let loose by dancing and having fun. We were not the only ones to participate in this ritual. There were many other dancers who would hit the park after clubbing all night long, and that's where the battles would ensue. Listen to this story...

One day at the park, this guy challenged me to a battle, popping. It was clear I was so much better than he was, but he wanted to continue. It seemed he had one more trick up his sleeve. It was a move where you would put a lit cigarette in your mouth and flip it backwards into your mouth, and then close your mouth and do a body wave, so it appeared you swallowed the cigarette. Well, this guy acted like he was the only one in the world who had ever done this trick with two lit cigarettes. I never did it with just one, I always did it with two cigarettes, but now I was not going to do the same thing he just did. So without ever trying it before, I decided to do it with three cigarettes!

Now despite popular opinion, I happen to have a very small mouth, so this was a challenge for me. But you see, I had always been the type of person who felt there was nothing I couldn't do if I wanted to. So I asked my crew member Tony to light the third cigarette for me. I was all ready to do my trick, and I did it! The crowd went wild. They gasped, and then the thunderous applause told my opponent he had been beaten. When I went to turn the cigarettes back out of my mouth, something horrible happened. Tony had given me a cigarette with a loose head on it, so it fell off of the cigarette and went right down my throat!

Well, I tried to expel it from my throat where it was burning me, but I couldn't. I tried to produce some more saliva to extinguish the burning head of the cigarette, but that did not work either. I really was concerned that I was going to have a hole burned in my throat. Finally my friend Tony got a soda from the vender standing just a few feet from us and I guzzled it. The funny thing was, it was a grape soda and I hate grape soda, but I think I would have drunk just about anything at that point.

That would not be the last time I hurt myself in Washington Square Park.

On another trip to the park after dancing all night, we all headed to the park, and there were a lot more of this time. A couple of guys from The Floor Masters were with us, and they happened to be brothers as well. Chino, Brian and Sammy had joined us for our dancing at the park ritual. I do not recall how it came to be, but we started displaying our gymnastic abilities. We were doing flips and back flips, and I wanted to do a back sumi, which is a backwards somersault in the air. Chino and Brian were spotting me, and I was just about to complete my last one when Chino was distracted and looked away. The next thing I knew, I hit the ground upside down between my head and my shoulder by my neck. I saw stars.

I really did!

Immediately I went to get up. I am a very proud person and I do not like to show weakness. But when I tried to sit up (I was lying on the ground on my back), I felt this searing pain shoot through my neck and my shoulder, and I quickly laid back down. My friend who has known me since I was fourteen knew something was wrong. She said "No, leave her. She must be really hurt because Kim doesn't lay back down." After a moment or two, I was able to get up. I remember having to sit on a big rock and just watch as everyone else continued to dance. Sammy, a.k.a. I.B. Samurai, one of the Floor Masters/Rockers Revenge, was there that day. He felt bad for me, and he sat behind me and tried to rub my shoulder. Every time he touched my shoulder, I saw those stars again. So do you think I went to the doctor's or a hospital? Of course not. Little did I know at the time I had broken my collarbone, which still sticks out to this day. I knew something was wrong because I couldn't shake it off, which is what I always do with pain.

For months I could not lift my arm. Every day I would try and lift it a little more. I had to have someone help me put my shirts on. If no one was home, I had to wear a button-down shirt. I do not recall how long it took me to finally be able to lift my arm high enough to put my shirt on myself, but I did it! I am not the only break dancer to ever get hurt, but I do believe I was the only one to lift two guys in the air with a broken collarbone, a torn rotator cuff, and torn ligaments in my left arm (I will get to that injury a little later).

The Fun House is where I also met a very special person who is not only a great friend, but is like a brother to me: Kano (Milton Torres). I met Kano and Susie before I had ever run into The Dynamic Rockers. The night I met The Dynamic Rockers at The Fun House was the same night I had spoken about earlier, where I was challenged for the name Spinner. The guys who had the same name was Elio, a member of The Dynamic Rockers. It was that night I was introduced to them and found out that Kano and Susie were members as well. As far as I was concerned, it was time to leave The Juice Crew and join a crew that was actually performing and getting paid. The Juice Crew had started off as a group of friends who loved to dance, and though they tried to become a professional dance crew, they were *not* breakers or poppers. With their blessings, I joined The Dynamic Breakers.

At first I was thrilled to be surrounded by so many talented breakers and poppers, and I was told we had to meet at this club in Manhattan to practice, because we would be doing a show there. My first real paying gig!

I took the train to Manhattan and found the club, called Playdough's Retreat. Now, I had no clue as to what kind of club this was until I got inside and took a look around. There was a big swimming pool in the middle of the place and a big round bed against a wall; some weird-looking contraptions here and there, and then a bar and a stage/dance floor. I did not see the rest of place until later, and then I knew exactly what kind of place this was. The guys told me it was a swingers' club, and although I knew what swingers were, I did not get the full understanding of what went on there until later.

I along with my friend Edna were going to be in this show with some of The Dynamic Rockers, There was no way all of the crew members could be in the show, for at that time there were about thirty-three of us, with many more to come. I helped Glyde (the president of The Dynamic Rockers) choreograph a routine which involved intricate lifts and a dance duet with me and Edna.

On a break, I also choreographed a dance routine for Susie Q and Gloria.

It was around that time that the overhead television sets turned on and there were porno movies being shown. I said, "What kind of place is this"? Susie Q laughed and said, "Come here, I want to show you something." I followed her to another part of the club and there was a long wall with many doors in it. It was like a huge cube that took up a tremendous area. Susie Q and Gloria opened one of the doors. All the while, they were giggling. I peeked inside and there was nothing but a mattress that took up the entire area of that little room.

They took me to a few more doors and I looked in those too. Each room was the same, only some were larger and some were smaller, depending upon the size of the orgy. These were sex and orgy rooms! I had never seen anything like this, nor did I know they existed. Now everything made sense—the large bed, and the weird machines that looked like twisted weight benches. I was out of there!

Okay, I did not leave. The guys talked me out of leaving. They assured me it was not bad at all. We would enter the stage by a back room so we would not have to walk through the club. And when we were finished, we left through those same doors and got paid, and then we left the club. Okay, I was not going to let some freaky people ruin my chance at my first paying gig.

The night had arrived. I always got anxious, not nervous, and I was anxious to get out there and do our thing. They announced us and the six of us came out on to the stage and took our places. At first I could not really see, for they had the spotlights shining on us and it was bright. When they music started, so did our dance routine. The first few maneuvers were done in pairs, so I was dancing with Glyde and Edna with Spyder. We jumped up and spun around their necks, and spiraled down their bodies until we came out from between their legs and slid forward onto the dance floor, which was when we stood up and faced the audience. That was when we got a good look at them.

Naked people! Naked people standing there, watching us perform. Now you see if you could remember your dance routine like ths! Somehow we did. There was this one part where Edna and I had to do a move where we slid past one another, crisscrossed each other across the dance floor. As we passed one another, we said, "Oh my God these people are naked" on the way back "Just don't look at them," I said. It was hard not to. There were men and women standing all around the stage. Some had the courtesy to wear a towel around their waists, but some just stood there au natural.

Old people, young people, and every age in between. The worst was that when they applauded, things jiggled! Loose skin and dangling body parts, jiggling everywhere. I could not wait to get off that stage and out of that place. You know how people say "just picture everyone in their underwear?" Not good advice! That was my first and my last performance at Playdough's Retreat.

Chapter 3—The Kennedy Center Honors

A huge opportunity was about to come my way. I'd received a phone call asking me if I would be interested in choreographing a large group of breakers for a show they would be performing at The Kennedy Center Honors in honor of Katherine Dunham, who was one of the five honorees that year. The Kennedy Center Honors is an annual show that chooses five talented people and honors their achievements with an award, a tribute performance, and a banquet dinner every year.

I was told that this performance would also be seen by the President of the United States, Ronald Regan. I was excited, but now as I look back on it, I realize what an honor and a once-in-a-lifetime opportunity it was. If you do not think it was a big deal, keep this in mind; I had no professional training and no credentials other than word of mouth. Being that there were no other crews who had really incorporated choreography into break dancing, I was the girl for the job. I had never worked with such a large group before, and I was still new.

I want to clear up one thing before we go any further; each dancer had their own moves. I choreographed a routine that incorporated each dancer's best moves, with timing to ensure everyone had the opportunity to get equal stage time. I also had to make sure our routine ended at the same exact time as our music. For instance, Wiggles and Fable used their pop/locking routine, and I made sure they kept it within the time frame needed. I did the same thing with all of the other dancers.

I remember I had to go to a large studio that overlooked Times Square, and when I entered the studio, I was very surprised at all of the different dancers that were there. We had some dancers from each prominent crew, including the NYC Breakers, the Rock Steady Crew, Magnificent Force, and of course, the Dynamic Dolls. I immediately got to work and made sure that every dancer had a solo. In addition, there were duos and all kinds of flow. People were moving at all times. During the first break we took, I was kidding around with the girls and I started to do a little popping and some floor moves. The people in charge of this were so impressed at my skills, they insisted that I join the show as one of the dancers as well.

It was so cool. I was sent out with the woman in charge of wardrobe to purchase an outfit for me. She informed me I could get whatever I wanted as long as it was purchased from The Gap, just like everyone else in the crew. It felt so cool to have someone purchase a new outfit for me. I remember feeling so official, like "this is show business." I also remember we all had to pass clearance, since we would be in the same vicinity as the President of the United States. The whole experience was amazing, and when we arrived at the hotel, we did not have just a regular room— we had a suite!

"We" were Susie Q, Coco Pop, Brenda K. Starr, and myself, "Kim-A-Kazi." We had a kitchen, living room, bedroom with two big beds, and a beautiful bathroom, as well as a walk-in closet. It was in that bathroom that I heard Brenda K. Starr sing "The Star Spangled Banner," a cappella and at my request. I had goose bumps. I was always a fan of Brenda's voice, and she really gives her all at every one of her performances.

One of the first famous people we met at the Westgate Hotel where we were staying was Florence Henderson, who you may know better as Mrs. Carol Brady from the 1970s television show "The Brady Bunch." She was staying on the same floor as we were, and it was in the elevator that we first met. Later during one of the rehearsals backstage in the theatre, I had come up with an idea. To make a long story short, I had taught Ms. Henderson how to do an arm wave. So when we exited the stage at the end of our performance, as we danced up the aisles, she would stand up and we would hold hands and do the "wave." The audience got a real kick out of seeing Mrs. Brady getting down with some popping skills. In the video which can be seen on YouTube, at the very end you can see me stop at the top of the screen and do the wave with her.

I will tell you, this was one amazing gig. We met some of the biggest stars in all of Hollywood: Mr. Gene Kelly, Carol Burnett, and of course, Katherine Dunham, whom we were honoring with our performance.

One day while we were practicing on the stage (the very one in the photo I have provided), we went through the entire performance and exited the stage to show everyone my idea of dancing off the stage and up the aisles, engaging the audience as we went by them. As I exited the stage and was running up the main aisle, I spotted the amazing Mr. Gene Kelly sitting a few rows back. He had been watching us rehearse. As I passed him while I was running up the aisle, I could not believe my eyes. He had been someone I had admired most of my life, and he was sitting there watching us dance and me choreographing.

Now, I make it a rule never to bother famous people. I mean I was on Regis Philbin's show twice and I never asked him for an autograph, nor did we pose for any pictures (I wish I did take more photographs, though). I was trying to decide what to do as I headed back down the aisle and toward the stage. I wanted to say something to him so badly, but I had such pride.

Finally, as I passed the row where he was seated, I called to him in little more than a whisper, "Mr. Kelly, Mr. Kelly." He turned and looked at me, and I blurted out, "You are such an inspiration to me." Then Mr. Gene Kelly spoke to me! He said "*You* are such an *inspiration* to me." What an amazing compliment. I did not know we would meet up again later.

But not all celebrities are so humble. For instance, after our performance at The Kennedy Center Honors, there was a huge banquet held afterwards. We had all gone to our suites to change from our dancing clothes into our formal wear. When we entered the banquet hall, it was massive. I cannot even explain to you how enormous it was, but there were large round tables with white tablecloths, and it looked as if we were at a royal wedding. Our table was all the way in the back of the room, so we had to pass just about every table, and there were many.

This was amazing! As we walked through the banquet hall, *every* table stood up and gave us another standing ovation. It was so surreal!

Now, I will not speak for everyone at our table, but as for myself, I had never been at such an elaborate affair. It was exactly how I imagined it would be. The food was more decorative than plentiful. You know how it is—you get this dinner plate, and in the center is some unrecognizable dish that resembles a work of art more than it does an entrée. We had certainly worked up an appetite, and even though I cannot tell you what we ate, I can tell you we were still hungry.

We all got up and went to mingle. I remember hitting the dance floor and there was nothing really exciting going on. There was an orchestra performing their rendition of hits from the '70s. I guess it was better than just sitting at our table. Many people came up to us to express how much they loved our performance. Then they all seemed to gang up on us. They were asking us to perform right there in our formal wear and to that elevator music the orchestra was playing. I was in a gown and high heels, so there was no way I was able to break dance, and I would look ridiculous popping in that outfit as well.

It was about that time I spotted Michael (the New York City Breaker's manager) from across the dance floor. He was talking to a group of people, and one of them was Lynda Carter, better known as Wonder Woman from her television show. I have a cousin who absolutely loved Lynda Carter and had Wonder Woman posters all over his bedroom. I thought how excited he would be if I got her autograph for him.

Now, I have already explained that I do not usually ask anyone for their autograph, but I have asked for autographs on behalf of family members. As a matter of fact, the day before while we were hanging out backstage after dress rehearsal, I happened to sit down on one of the sofas next to Geoffrey Holder. He was such a nice man, and we had a conversation which made me comfortable enough to ask him for his autograph for my aunt, who loved him. I have a memory of posing for a picture with him, but I don't know who took it. Mr. Holder just passed away in October 2014. He was best known for his deep baritone voice, which he used for his 7Up commercials back in the day, "The Un-Cola." Some may know him from Broadway, and some from his many films, including "Annie," Live and Let Die," and "Doctor Doolittle." He was 84 years old.

Being that Michael Hollman was already speaking to Lynda Carter, it would be a perfect way to be introduced and work the autograph politely into the conversation. I made my way across the dance floor and joined the small group talking to her. When Michael finished his conversation, he introduced me to the small group. Immediately after Michael and two other men walked away, I was left there with Lynda and a man who I assumed was her husband. After a few polite compliments regarding her show, I went for it. "Ms. Carter, I never would think to bother anyone when they are at a party, but —" That was as far as I got before she began screaming at me.

"I hope you aren't going to ask me for an autograph, how dare you..." and blah, blah, blah.

I have no idea what she said to me after those few words, because I saw white! Some people see red, some black out, but I see white. With her screaming loudly in front of the entire room and pointing her bony finger at me—well that was all it took. I began screaming back at her, and all I remember saying was that I would beat her face in with her own wonder tits, I would use them as punching bags and blacken both her eyes and knock her teeth out with them, or something along those lines.

What I do remember is seeing Michael Hollman's face as he saw me yelling at Lynda Carter—he had a look of shock and horror. Now there is no mistaking my mood, because my face does not lie, especially when I am angry. When Michael saw my face and came running over, he told me I had better get out of there before she called security and I got ejected. So I did.

After seeing how tight security was due to the President and the First Lady, I wasn't taking any chances. Not the kind of impression you want following your career.

Throughout this book you will read several stories similar to this one, because I do not consider anyone to be above me. I will not allow any person to look down on me just because they have a career in show business. I will not be mistreated or spoken down to by anyone!

The night of our performance, everyone was buzzing around backstage, I remember we were in this huge room with rows and rows of those mirrors with the lights around them, which is where most of the performers were having their makeup done. It was in this room that my conversation with Gene Kelly began as we waited for our turn to have our makeup done.

Brenda K. Starr came down the main hallway, and she looked a little upset. She proceeded to tell a few of us that she was excited when she spotted Mikhail Baryshnikov, the famous ballet dancer. Brenda spoke to him and she says he told her this: "I would not expect a real response from the audience, for what you do is nothing more than a fad. What I do is an art." Now I think that is a real crappy and immature thing to say to a kid who is about to perform in front of the President of the United States, the First Lady, and Hollywood's most elite. Keep in mind, some of us were still kids, and this was a huge opportunity for all of us. But there is a happy ending, people.

After our performance, we received a standing ovation! The only other person who received a standing ovation that evening was Anthony Quinn for Zorba the Greek.

I wholeheartedly believe in karma, and Mr. Baryshnikov got a taste of karma that night. In the upcoming photo of the Kennedy Center Honors performance, you can see some of the audience beginning to stand. We have a photo of the entire audience standing, but who knows what happened to that one? What was great about the whole scenario was, Mr. Baryshnikov went on right before we did, and although the audience clapped for him, they did not get up out of their seats and give him a standing ovation as they had done for us. I'm sure he felt like a real idiot after that. Ha ha!

(right to left) Brenda K Starr, Coco Pop, Susie Q; 1983 – Washington

NYC Breakers & Dolls in Washington (I took the photo) 1983

Matthew (A.K.A. Glyde Master) from the NYC Breakers–@ practice. We lost Matthew the following year when he was killed by a drunk driver.... RIP

The Dynamic Dolls & the Wonderful Carol Burnett

Brenda K. Starr, Susie & Kim-A-Kazi – Washington '83

We received a standing ovation! Kennedy Center Honors 1983. My face is blocked—I am center stage in the red, white and black shirt near Susie Q in the pink pinstriped pants.

The Dynamic Dolls Meet Dancing Legend Gene Kelly

Gene Kelly's autograph –We spent over an hour talking to one another.

Susie Q (left) and Kim-A-Kazi (right) during our duo

Note: The Dynamic Dolls performed duets, solos, and there was a battle: Kim-A-Kazi and Susie Q against Brenda K.

Starr and Coco Pop. All of our performances were cut from the televised performance. Once again, the B-Girls are swept under the rug.

I would like to say that all of the dancers who were in this performance deserve credit. Before going on stage, I realized they had put new props on the stage that interfered with our original entrance. I immediately told everyone that we had to change our entrance. Everyone adapted to the new entrance like a pro.

Also during our performance, one of the dancers got a little carried away with their solo and took up more time than they were supposed to. Because the entire performance had been choreographed to end with the music, this person threw the entire performance off. The other dancers had to make up the time. I did not want them to miss out on their performance, so I just urged them to speed it up just a little.

The difference can be noticed at the very end of our performance, when the orchestra had to chime in and give us a little help for the last few seconds. I wish I could find the raw footage to that performance, as well as all of the others that our best moves or our complete performances were edited out.

The Body Mechanix

Again, we would have to return to The Fun House. My popping skills were really improving rapidly, and this one night I was dancing and I started popping. Immediately I drew a crowd. It was a rare sight to see a female popping and doing it well, and to see a white female was virtually unheard of, but nevertheless seen. I noticed these guys in the crowd who were all dressed in black and wearing white gloves.

When I was done, I continued to freestyle dance. This very tall guy approached me, along with the guys with the white gloves. First he complimented me on my skills and expressed that he was blown away. He then introduced himself to me as Nelson Cruz. We shook hands and, then he introduced the guys behind him as "The Body Mechanix," a crew from the Bronx.

The few guys from the crew that had seen me do my thing were totally down with having me join their crew. However, the other crew members that had not gone to The Fun House that evening were like, "Say what? A white girl—are you crazy?" Needless to say, I was not received with open arms when I arrived in the Bronx for our first practice.

Yep, two and a half hours on the subways from Brooklyn to the boogie-down Bronx. I must tell you, I got more crazy looks and stares from every person that saw me. I mean, not for nothing—here I was, a skinny white girl all dressed up in Hip Hop style, not too bad looking either, and walking down the streets of the Bronx all by myself. These people must have figured I was a crazy lady, because they looked, but most of them never said one word to me. But I didn't care. I was there for a reason, and as far as I was concerned, I grew up in a very mixed neighborhood so I was comfortable no matter where I went.

I even got my picture in the New York Post newspaper, because I was on the platform waiting for the train at three o'clock in the morning in the Bronx on my way home to Brooklyn. I had been in the Bronx all day long practicing, and I never had the chance to read my newspaper from that day. So there I was standing on the platform, all alone reading my paper, when these three people cautiously approached me. They were from the New York Post—what a coincidence. Anyway, they asked me why I wasn't afraid and all these other questions, and you can see the original article on the next page.

Okay, back to practicing. So the first day I showed up, the guys from The Body Mechanix may have been reluctant when they met me, but when they saw me pop they were sold.

I will try and say this the best way I can without sounding conceited, because I do not have too many people who are willing to put their testimonials in print. We began to practice and here I was fairly new to popping, yet to my own surprise I immediately began to choreograph a routine for me and the guys. They were impressed and I was very proud of myself, and I guess it just goes to show that some people have a natural ability. Not all dancers can choreograph, and not all dancers can teach.

Our manager, Mr. Nelson Cruz, was also a brilliant musician and music producer and was working on a few new songs for Shannon, who sang "Let the Music Play" and "Give Me Tonight," along with many other songs.

One day Nelson's partner, Chris Barbossa (another musical genius), was giving me a lift back to Brooklyn and he said to me, "Hey, I am working on this new song. Would you tell me what you think?"

I told him I'd be honored to. Now, I do not know why so many artists have asked my opinion regarding their music, because I am not a musician and I do not know much about music, except for what I like. Anyway Chris popped in a cassette, and I listened to the music. I loved it! It was slamming, and even though I loved the hard beats and the bass, I felt like they were a little too much and somewhat overpowering. That was my opinion.

Regardless of my opinion, they had another hit on their hands Chris Barbossa is a very talented man and a great person. We too have recently been reunited thanks to the Internet. Shannon told me not long ago that she asked Chris to come back into the business, but he is happy in what he is doing. Shannon said Chris was a musical genius, and I concur.

The biggest news to hit the streets was all about this huge break dance contest that would be taking place at The Roxy night club in Manhattan and, it was going to be televised.

First prize was to appear in the new break dance movie "Beat Street." People and crews came from all over, far and wide, to audition for this contest. I cannot recall why at this time, but the only ones who performed and made it to the semi-finals were three members of The Body Mechanix: me, Kevin, and a girl named Dee who had recently joined our crew. That would be the last time I would be a member of The Body Mechanix.

The reporters were so stunned that I was riding the subway all alone at 3 a.m. in the Bronx. There were three of them, and they looked scared to death. There wasn't anything that could keep me from dancing.

In Memory of "Jackie"

At this very time I was hanging out with Pablo and Richie Rock, because I had become good friends with a woman Pablo was dating. It reminds me a little of the movie "Breakin'," where the older white girl dates the street dancer, except Jackie was way more than a few years older than Pablo. She was in her thirties and had a five-year-old little girl back then. Jackie was separated from her husband and had just gotten her own apartment.

We spent a lot of time together, and I was going to spend a couple of days with her helping to get her apartment in order. We went shopping and all got the same outfits, then I picked up some of my own groceries, since I would be there for a few days.

That night we were all going to The Roxy, where they were going to make an announcement about the upcoming "Big Break Dance Contest," the very first televised one. All of a sudden I became terribly ill, which is a very rare event. I had things shooting out of me from all ends! Never had this ever happened to me before, and there was no way I could go out that night.

Everyone was so disappointed, so they did what they could to help me feel better, and after a while I felt that I could make it out.

We weren't at The Roxy very long when I became sick again and spent half the night in the ladies' room. I told Jackie that I had to go home back to Brooklyn. Jackie insisted I go back to her apartment in Queens, and she would take care of me. She reminded me I had left all my new clothes and groceries there. I told her I would come back as soon as I felt better in a day or two. There was no way I could take the subway home, so I hailed a cab and prayed I would make it home without getting sick again.

The next morning I felt fine, good as new, so I went out to do a few errands. When I got back home, my aunt was on the phone and she looked strange (since my mom threw me out, I lived with my aunt for a little while). She handed me the receiver and said it's Nelson. I got on the phone, and Nelson said, "Kim, I have some bad news." I said, "Oh, let me guess. The tour you said we were going on with Michael Jackson is not happening, right?"

He said, "Jackie is dead."

I dropped the phone, and it fell to the floor. I could not believe what I had just been told, but it was true. What happened was that very day, Jackie decided to go to her ex-husband's house to pick up a few of her daughter's belongings. Jackie's ex owned a restaurant/pizzeria and she thought he would be at work, but he had not been to his place of business for over three weeks. He had lain in wait with a sawed-off shotgun at his home for Jackie to show up. When she arrived, he killed her, and then turned the gun on himself.

Anyone who knows me, knows that if I had slept over at Jackie's as planned, I would have definitely gone with her to her ex-husband's house to help her—and maybe I would have been killed as well. I was made to be sick because I was not meant to be there, just as certain events took place to ensure that Pablo and Richie were not there, either.

It was a very sad time for everyone, especially that little girl. She had lost her mommy and her daddy that day. I have never been sick like that, before or after that fateful day, and I believe that is when my spiritual growth began. I introduced Pablo and Richie Rock to The Body Mechanix, and they became crew members as I was about to leave my crew.

Chapter 4—Becoming a Dynamic Breaker

The night of the finals of The Big Break Dance Contest was filmed at The Roxy. Carlos DeJesus was the host. He was a popular radio personality whom most of us had been listening to on the radio, 92 WKTU, for years. Also hosting was the famous dancer Ms. Leslie Ugums. The celebrity judges were Hershel Walker, professional football hero; and Debbie Morgan and Darnel Williams, stars of the soap opera "All My Children." Just to show you how new and inexperienced the outside world was to Hip Hop, not one of the judges was a professional dancer or knew anything about break dancing. Can you imagine holding the biggest break dance contest in the world and hiring judges who knew nothing about break dancing? It would never happen today.

Most every crew we had ever heard of was there, including my former crew, The Dynamic Rockers. So we (The Body Mechanix) were next to perform at the finals. We had made it all the way through to the finals, and I was standing there waiting for our music to begin so we could come down the aisle and get on stage to perform. All of a sudden, the wrong music came blasting over the speakers. This wasn't any music I had ever heard before, and certainly was not something we could perform to.

Mr. Carlos DeJesus began yelling at us to "come on, let's go." I was telling him that was not our music. You see, I had choreographed a popping routine to Shannon's song "Let the Music Play" as a tribute to our manager, Nelson Cruz. Each pop and tick and wave were set to each beat of the song, adding to the dramatics of the moves. I was not trying to be difficult—we just wanted our music. But he threw such a fit. He was screaming at us over his microphone to just get up there and dance anyway. I refused and told him we needed our music, or it would greatly affect our performance. He yelled back at me, "Well, if you were a professional, you could dance to anything," and I yelled back to him, "Well, if you were so professional, you would be playing the correct music."

I don't really remember what was said after that. I do remember my crew telling me to be quiet and stop arguing with the host, but that is the way I was. I did not care who you were. If you got nasty, loud and disrespectful with me, I got that way with you. I also have a very bad temper, and when I get angry I lose my mind and sometimes black out from things that I have said and done while in that state. I have worked on that over the years.

So finally they straightened things out and played our music, and we did our thing. After our performance, a bunch of people came up to me giving me props on my skills, and some of those people happened to be my friends and fellow crew members from The Dynamic Rockers. I noticed they were not wearing the same red and blue satin outfits that The Dynamic Rockers had worn. They had on these kick-ass outfits that had The Dynamic Breakers in graffiti. They told me that they had left The Dynamic Rockers and started a new crew, The Dynamic Breakers. Since Spyder, Kano, Airborne and Flip were all original members of Dynamic Rockers and helped to create the crew, they were entitled to take the Dynamic name with them when they left.

They had added one other guy, Duce, a guy who could spin on his head forever if he wanted to. Also, there were my girls, Susie Q and Brenda K. Starr. They asked me if I would join their crew, and although I really like The Body Mechanix, I knew this was something big. I mean, they had the cream of the crop, and once they got on that stage and began to perform, it was evident. I knew right there and then that The Dynamic Breakers were going to win that contest, and I think everyone else did as well.

I had gone over to these booths and tables they had there at The Roxy. You see, The Roxy was originally a roller skating rink, and they still had the rental counter and the food counter where you could buy something to eat. I was sitting in a booth talking to one of my friends who were in The Dynamic Rockers when the president of TDR came over to me. He started telling me how amazing I had gotten, and he asked me to rejoin TDR. I told Glyde (the president of The Dynamic Rockers) that I appreciated his offer, but I had just joined up with The Dynamic Breakers. He did not like that at all, so he decided to threaten me.

He told me that if I did not decide right there to rejoin his crew, he was going to tell these females to beat my ass. I looked and there were about seven females rocking these sheepskin coats, posing in a B-Boy stance. Now, I am not the kind of person you can threaten. As I told you before, I am too spiteful and prideful to back down from anyone. No matter how many there were. Heck, I had forty-five males and females come after me back in my neighborhood in Brooklyn, and I did not care! I still turned around and cursed all of them out. I am not trying to sound all bad—it is just the way I am, I will not be bullied, and I won't allow bullying to go on in my presence, no matter what.

Well, that was it, I stood up from the booth and said, "Let's go, bring it on." When none of the girls made a move, I walked away. Hey, I am no fool I was prepared, waiting for a mob of females to jump me from behind, but they did not. And that was how I became a Dynamic Breaker, The best break dance crew in the world. And here is why...

Me with two other members of The Body Mechanix @ the Big Break Dance Contest at The Roxy in NYC (That's me in the pink)

The Dynamic Breakers, The Best Break Dance Crew in the World

The Dynamic Breakers: Kano, Flip, Airborne, Spyder, and Duce, with Kim-A-Kazi and Susie Q. The cream of the crop.

I had known Kano and Susie the longest, but when I learned that they all had left the Dynamic Rockers and then added Duce to become The Dynamic Breakers, I knew that this was going to be the best crew in existence.

I could have been with just about any crew I wanted to, so I do not want you to think I am being biased here. Dynamic was the best—not only because of their amazing skills or their diversity, but because they were so funny and added comedy into their routines.

Routines—did you get that word? Now I told you I have been choreographing since I was little, but Dynamic was the only crew back then that incorporated choreography into their performances (break dance crew, that is, for I know there were crews like The Lockers from Cali and a few other Pop-Lockers that put together routines). But as for break dance crews, all the others would stand back, and one guy would walk up and do his moves, and then just walk back in line, Dynamic was always moving. We had routines going on in the background (not so much that it took away from what was going on up stage) and when it was time for the next person or duo to head to the front of the stage, we had "transition" moves, so no one was ever just walking around on the stage. You all know you can't perform or battle today without having a choreographed routine, as well as tricks and crowd-pleasers, and that all started with Dynamic (Rockers, Breakers and Dolls).

What also put us far above the rest was that we spent countless hours practicing. Now, I am not trying to say that no other crews practiced. But they did not have any choreography, so they practiced moves. Dynamic practiced routines and creating new moves, and we tried to never go out and do the same old stuff every time—unlike some other crews, who once they gained a little fame never strived to get any better or improve their skills. Despite their inability to win any contests or battles, this crew went on to be the most well-known crew in the world.

Some say they rode on the coattails of those who had made it big from their neighborhood, and that could be true. For out of all of the crews out there, they would not even make the list of the top 20 as far as skills. But they did something that most all the other crews did not. They kept themselves out there.

When break dancing started dying out, The Dynamic Breakers went on, and each one achieved great heights away from entertaining (I will get to that later). Some B-Boys took it overseas where Hip Hop was really beginning to grow, and these people were smart and took full advantage of that. I think that was a smart move on their part.

What really pisses me off, though, is all of the lies some people are spewing. They have been traveling around the world for decades teaching Hip Hop history, but they tell lies. Not only to make themselves seem more important and better than they really were, but to speak such lies against others—especially me and The Dolls.

That is a disgrace, and there should be something done to stop anyone from being paid or getting up in front of people and falsifying the facts of history. The funny part is, one guy said to an audience of people that "there were no B-girls back in the day, I don't care what you may have heard." He tells them this, which really makes him look foolish—especially when there is video showing us performing together!

I have an e-mail from this guy's sister saying, "Oh, my brother taught me all about The Dynamic Dolls, and he said that you, Kim-A-Kazi, *had crazy dope skills.*" I'd never had a problem with this person.

It is sad that as adults, these people are still displaying the same juvenile behavior they did back as kids. It all stems from egos and the fear that the truth will be revealed, and their lies will be uncovered. I don't blame them for being afraid and for trying to do anything to keep the truth quiet. I know if I had been lying for years, I would be concerned too. They had to know the truth would eventually come out. That's what people do when they feel the truth about them isn't good enough. I do not lie or feel that I need to exaggerate about anything I did. Everything I say can be proven.

It is sad what some people will do to try to gain a little fame. The only reason I would want to gain a little recognition for my contributions is that it would give me a little more leverage with my goal to go around to schools and speak to the children. I know I can do that, but having a title like "Hip Hop Hall of Fame Inductee" not only gives me an edge, it can also give me an instant connection with these children. Something they can relate to, other than having some adult lecturing them.

We may not have been as famous back then as many celebrities, but we got just enough of a taste of what it's like to be a celebrity that some people just could not accept returning to a life a being just a regular person. I understand that the "star treatment" can be difficult to let go of.

We were treated like celebrities—limousines picking you up, wardrobe and makeup people fussing over you, photographers taking your pictures for major magazines. Anything you want to eat was brought to you. Staying in luxury hotels, fans chasing you for your autograph, it can all be very alluring. Some people will do whatever it takes to try to hold onto or recapture all of that.

Me? I feel lucky and blessed that I was able to have those experiences at all, and I will cherish those memories always. Fame is not something I covet. For instance, I would love to become an actress because of the art, the expression, but never for the fame. I would never want to be hounded all the time, in all of the tabloids. Some people need that kind of attention, and that is okay for them—but for me, not so much.

We all worked hard and fought to make Hip Hop become a culture, and we fought against discriminations that we all faced in the beginning. Someone said to me, "Man, how amazing would it be to have the three major crews from back in the day all together on a television show or something?" I am doubtful that would ever happen. Maybe two of us, but not all three. But who knows? Stranger things have happened. I think it would be a positive message showing that Hip Hop can bring all people together, even rivals.

Seriously, I find it all so silly. You know we are not going to live forever, and I feel it would be a great piece of Hip Hop history to do a show or a documentary with the main crews of our day

Now, back to Dynamic!

I cannot recall at this time what my first performance was as a Dynamic Breaker. Heck, I can't even recall half of our performances, for there were so many. It seems like my dancing career happened in a short amount of time, but it was jam-packed. Every day we had somewhere to go, some people to see, something to do. Besides performances, we also did a lot of radio shows. We would go to radio stations like WBLS, KISS FM and WKTU, to name a few, and we would do a promo spot. We would announce who we were and promote the radio station. We also did a few shows for the radio stations out and around the city.

One show, we did for WBLS near the Burlington building, where they had a stage built. This was just The Dynamic Dolls performing. After the show as we were exiting the stage, a man approached me. He was impeccably dressed, and he introduced himself as Michael D. Klein, vice president of program development for Twentieth Century Fox Television. He told me he was in NYC from Beverly Hills, California, and he was interested in The Dolls for an upcoming TV sitcom. As usual, I took everything in stride, I took his card and he informed me when to call him. I was excited, but it was like anything else—nothing more than a consideration. Nothing was final until somebody signed the check.

When you can't trust the very people you pay to further your career, what do you do? I tried to contact Michael D. Klein many times by telephone, and he was always out of the office or in a meeting. I always said I would call him back, because I was wary of giving them the phone number to "Headquarters."

Headquarters was what we called our manager's place of business. He and his family owned and operated a printing store in Manhattan. It was also where he ran Break Dance International, which was our company and where anyone who was interested in The Dynamic Breakers and The Dynamic Dolls would call. I did not want this man from Twentieth Century Fox to speak to my manager, Cord Hamilton, because I had started to realize that Cord was not doing things for The Dynamic Dolls that were in our best interests. Maybe if I had trusted our managers, we could have set up a deal with Twentieth Century Fox and had our own sitcom. I will get back to the whole trust issue in a little while, for you will hear many examples of the deceit that went on within our little happy break dance family.

The beginning of The Dynamic Dolls–Kim-A-Kazi and Susie Q

Kim-A-Kazi and Susie Q practicing on outdoor stage in Italy

Kim-A-Kazi and Susie Q practicing on outdoor stage in Italy

So many stories to tell—too many stories to tell. It is not always easy trying to figure out which ones will entertain people or have that history factor that many second or third generations of Hip Hop enthusiasts look for. So I think what I will do is just chill and tell you some stories and facts I think you will enjoy, without worrying about writing everything in the order of which it occurred.

Let's get to the good stuff.

Chapter 5—Beat Street the Movie

I can only remember bits and pieces about the audition, but I do remember it was really a mere formality—because I already heard that they wanted Dynamic in the movie, and of course The Dynamic Breakers were the winners of the big break dance contest at the Roxy, with the prize being a part in the film Beat Street.

I remember we (The Dynamic Dolls) walked in to the place where the auditions were being held. The first thing I saw was ballet and jazz dancers all over the place. There were dancers stretching on the floors, and a very long line where they waited to audition. As we passed the long line of dancers, I was very confused. Tights, leg warmers, capezios—what were these dancers doing auditioning for a movie about Hip Hop? Once we saw the movie, we understood.

We did not have to wait in any lines, and I must say we kind of became spoiled, because we never waited in any line for anything any longer. I remember walking past the dancers waiting in line and there was a large clearing where the dancers were auditioning. Sitting in a chair with a team of people all around him was Mr. Harry Belafonte. He is the man everyone had to audition for. We stood there for no more than a minute before we were directed to dance, just a few feet from Harry Belafonte.

I am so proud of my girls, because none of us ever got nervous or had stage fright. We just got out there and did our thang, each and every time. Mr. Belafonte was leaning back in his chair, to the point that he teetered on just the two back legs of the chair. I remember thinking to myself as I was dancing that I hoped he did not fall. He seemed to enjoy our performance very much, for he had a huge smile on his face throughout most of our performance. And that was it—we left.

When it was decided that Dynamic would not be able to do the movie, The Dolls were still asked to be in the movie as dancers. I was the only Doll that showed up that day to the bus that was to take us to the location in the Bronx where we would be filming. I had hoped the girls would meet me there, being that JaeCie live in the Bronx and Susie Q lived in Harlem, but I soon realized I was on my own.

Once we reached our destination, many of us were instructed to remain on the bus until we were summoned. I was on the bus with two females I knew who were going to be used as background/people in the crowd, Josie and Peaches. Josie had been asking me what happened to the other Dolls and if I thought they would show up tomorrow. I knew she was hoping they wouldn't. Finally I was called off the bus, and I was instructed to walk into the building with some other females. We were on our way to the Jam they had going on in the abandoned building. And yes, it was really an abandoned, broken-down building. As the hours crawled by it became dark outside, and even colder. All we had for heat was that garbage can with a fire in it outside the building that you see in the movie. After thirteen and a half hours in the cold, I was done.

That is where you see me in the movie, somewhere after the first five minutes into the movie. We must have walked up and down, in and out, back and forth about a hundred times! Either the cable was not thrown out of the window at the correct time, or there was a mess up with the actors walking below the cables being thrown. Hours had passed before we all finally made it inside the building. I was taken upstairs and placed right at the doorway where the party was going on. I was with a guy who was standing real close to me, and we were supposed to be talking as the main characters came up the stairs and into the party.

For those of you who have never been a part of a movie, commercial or television program, I must tell you it can be very embarrassing. You feel very foolish at times. We had to have one of those fake conversations where you act like you are speaking to one another, but you cannot utter a sound.

50

As the actors are coming up the stairs, they have dialog, so the microphones have to pick up their conversation and nobody else's. Plus, me and the guy they paired me with were trying so hard not to laugh because—if they'd left it in, you would have seen for yourself—I was the whitest person there, and he was the darkest!! You just had to see us next to one another, and we were cracking jokes about it.

Finally we were getting to the good part—the dancing! I was so ready to get busy dancing, popping, and I was going to hit the floor, too. Just as we started filming the dance scene: "Cut! That's a rap for today. We will pick up again tomorrow."

But for me there was no tomorrow, and I knew those two females could not have been happier. When I told Josie I was probably not returning, she found it impossible to hide her excitement. How I regret not showing up again the next day, or any of the other days, because I could have been all over that movie, and all of you would be able to see my real skills—not the few moves that some inexperienced editor left in or cut out. If people could see me at my best, I think everyone would be blown away by my skills. Oh well, what are you going to do? Who knew that three decades later, the movie would be iconic? That is why I bring this movie up in my regrets chapter.

I was happy for all of my friends who were in the movie, especially Robert (Robert Taylor, who played Lee) and The NYC Breakers, who definitely won that battle with TRSC. I always liked Chino (Action) as a B-Boy. He had nice skills and a really good voice. When we were all together in Washington, Chino was singing—and what a voice. Every time to this day I hear "Joanna" by Kool and The Gang, it reminds me of him because of how beautiful he sang it.

Beat Street also makes me sad because we lost Matthew "Glide Master" shortly after filming to a drunk driver. I attended his services and burial, and I will never forget how grief-stricken his mother was, understandably. He was only a teenager. I think he was sixteen. I remember the night when the NYC Breakers came into the Roxy and I saw them making their way through the crowded dance floor, leaning in to say something to certain people as they went by. When they came to us and I heard the terrible news, I was stunned. I am glad I have a few photos of Glide Master to share with you in this book.

Kim-A-Kazi (center); Beat Street the movie. Me entering the building where the party takes place

Peek-A Boo! I see me to the left. This was the scene I was just telling you about, having the pretend conversation at the party.

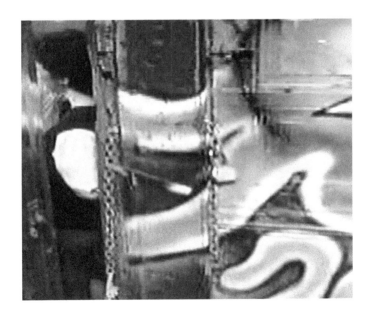

Chapter 6—A Once in a Lifetime Historical Event

The 1984 Swatch Watch Fresh Fest tour definitely fits under this title. However, it is an event that occurred before the tour even began. The lineup of talent consisted of several major rap artists and several dance crews. I will list them for you.

Rap Artists: Newcleus, Whodini, The Fat Boys, Kurtis Blow, and RunDMC

Dancers: Swatch Breakers, Uptown Express, Fantastic Duo, and of course, The Dynamic Breakers. The Dynamic Dolls made several guest performances at my insistence.

It was the first day of the tour and we were all to meet in Manhattan, New York City, where a Greyhound bus was waiting for us. It was the only time we would all be together on the same bus, for once we arrived in the first city on the tour, each headliner got their own tour bus complete with all the amenities you would get at a hotel. We had a living room with a TV, VCR and a mini fridge, and two couches. We had 12-16 sleeper compartments, a bathroom, and a back room with a table and an extra bed. We had a lot of fun on that tour bus.

So all of the entertainers I mentioned above loaded onto this Greyhound bus, and off we went. Every stop the bus made for gas, we would all pile out and go in for some snacks. For some reason, before long it seemed everyone else had eaten all their snacks and drank all their drinks, so they would come poking around Kim-A-Kazi, knowing I was a junk food junkie. As a matter of fact, Run (Joe Simmons, now known as Rev Run) used to come snooping around my seat looking for some Pepsi. "I'll pay ya back at the next stop," he would promise, but I was happy to share. I even bought extra snacks in case someone got hungry in between stops. So with a long road trip ahead and people getting bored, we all started doing what came naturally to us. The dancers got up in the aisles and busted a few moves; the rappers all seemed to be wearing a Walkman and listening to music.

One of the members of UTFO was always trying to hit on me, and with nowhere to run, he used to trap me in my seat all the time. Well, he was getting a little out of hand when Doc Ice came over and saved me. Doc and I got to be friends. I liked him from the first time we met, and we are still friendly today. Anyway, as Doc sat next to me, he asked me if I would listen to their new song. Doc told me they were starting their own group called UTFO, and they made this new song down in the basement. He slipped the cassette in the radio and pressed the "Play" button.

I listened to their recording, and when it was done, Doc looked at me anxiously awaiting my response. I told him "Yo, you guys got a serious hit on your hands. That song is going to kill." And it did. For those of you who haven't guessed it yet. the song he played for me was "Roxanne–Roxanne." Doc Ice is still making music, and his stuff is off the hook. It has a new sound, but with old-school flavor. You should check out his latest hits. Doc also crossed over into the fragrance business, coming out with his own cologne called "Karat."

The best is still to come.

So with all of these talented people all on one bus, it would seem inevitable that someone was going to start rapping. I have to tell you, it was amazing!

We would start from the front of the bus and go back row by row, switch to the other side of the bus and go row by row back up to the front, then start all over. One person at a time had to rap two lines, and then the next person had to pick it up from there and put in his two lines, and so on and so on. Man, it was crazy!

All of these legends on one bus, matching wits. It was not only magical, it was *historical*. How I wish someone would have recorded it, but we did not have cell phones like today when people record everything. If that was the case, I would have footage of me and the Dolls all over the place, and you all can see how *amazing* we were for real. The few things we do have on video are edited pieces and do not show our real talent. I will hit on that subject in a minute. I want to finish telling you a few things about the Fresh Fest tour first.

One of the things I loved to do during that tour was collect all of the day time tickets to the concert. Each performer would receive a couple of free tickets for each performance; we would do a day time show and a night time show on Friday, Saturday and Sunday. I would trade my night time tickets to the guys for their day time tickets. The guys like to invite the ladies to the night show and then chill with them later, so they were happy to give up their day tickets for night tickets, especially when they found out what I was doing with them.

I would go outside to the back of the line of people who were waiting to get in. No matter which state or what city we were in, there would always be a bunch of kids hanging around, wishing they could attend the show. I mean, this was the biggest show there was, and there was always a packed house wherever we went. I'm talking stadiums, not little theaters. Stadiums that held 25 to 50 thousand people. I would start a conversation with the kids, and they were usually very excited when I told them who I was and what crew I was with. I would ask them why they weren't coming to the show. They often said they didn't have the money for the tickets. I would then ask them if they lived nearby. They usually did: "right up the block," many of them told me. Then I would ask, "If I gave you a pair of tickets to the show today would you be able to bring me back a note from an adult saying you can attend?"

And that's when the kids would lose their minds. Some would check to see if I was playing with them. One boy almost got hit by a car trying to run home and get permission. After that, I had to make sure they went carefully and I watched them, I promised them I would wait for them to return. I loved, loved, loved doing that. Boy, those kids were out of their minds with joy. When the guys found out what I was doing with the tickets they, all gave up their day time tickets, no problem.

Unfortunately I did not get to do that for the whole tour—because you see, I was nothing more than a stand-in for Flip, one of The Dynamic Breakers. Flip had broken his foot, and I was the only other one who could spin a guy on my head and spin two guys in the air, and I knew all of our routines—plus I was the only one who could really pop, something that the guys were missing. Anyway, as soon as Flip healed I was out. Wouldn't you know, the very first weekend that Flip was back and I was out, Whodini filmed their video *"The Freaks Come Out at Night,"* and everyone else on that tour was in the video? I always missed out.

There was one little boy on the tour who was one of the dancers. He had these cute curls, and he could hold the audience. Here is a picture of that little boy. Can you guess who he is?

One day I was talking to Charles Stettler who is The Fat Boys' manager, I was standing in their hotel room and the front door was wide open. As we were talking, a pizza delivery guy came into the room with a stack of boxes with hot fresh pizza. I kid you not—Buffy, Prince and Kool all came barreling into the room at top speed. Charles and I were standing directly in the path between them and the table where the pizzas were set down. Thank goodness I was slim and quick, because I got out of the way just in time. I was invited to stay and join them, but I was not getting between those boys and their food!

Can you guess who this is?

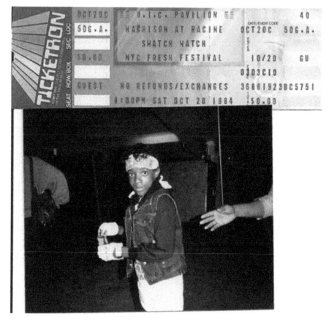

Jermaine Dupree - was on the Fresh Fest tour 1984

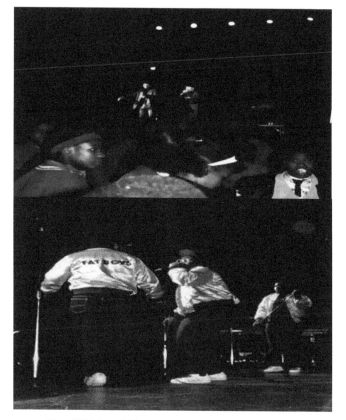

Run DMC and The Fat Boys at Fresh Fest 1984

Being the only female on the entire tour was okay. The guys were pretty respectful and treated me as part of the gang. There were times when it was a little lonely. The days were always busy with preparing for the shows, but night time was really boring for me because, the guys would be out with some groupies, and there were always females trying to get with anyone who was in the show. Not much for me to do, being the only female. Plus I did not drink, so even if there were some of the guys who were married or had girlfriends that were not "getting lucky" and were hanging out at the bar, it was not my scene. Many of my nights were spent alone in my room.

I remember this one night, it was a Sunday night after the show and we had packed our suitcases on the bus, so we were ready to head back to New York right after the show was over. I was waiting in our tour bus with the driver. We waited and waited and I was getting annoyed, because I was anxious to get home. Finally the guys showed up with a crowd of females following them. Some of the guys who were single took a female and went into the bed area. I sat up front with the driver and waited some more. Finally they escorted the females off the bus, and I was like "finally we can leave," but I was wrong. Next! They picked out some more girls and headed to the back of the bus. The bus was rocking and I was fuming. Finally when things quieted down, I was fed up, I went back to the bed area, ripped open the door and started yelling. I cannot tell you exactly what I said, but I know it was something like, "I want all you sluts off this frigging bus now." (Excuse my language but I was tired and cranky).

It is crazy how people act around celebrities and performers. I understand it can be exciting to meet someone you have admired, as I did with Mr. Gene Kelly. However, I did not launch myself at the man and proceed to tear his clothes from his body.

I guess "groupies" are a whole different kind of fan, and there was never a short supply of screaming females all trying to make it with the guys. I myself got a few propositions from a few guys, but I wasn't interested.

Being on tour was amazing, but there were a few downsides to it, at least for me. One thing about going on tour is you travel all over the world, yet you really do not get to see much or enjoy the surroundings, because you're always busy. If we were not performing on stage, we were doing promotions for the shows or interviews—but most of the time we were traveling.

Kim-A-Kazi @ Fresh Fest '84 with The Dynamic Breakers

Dynamic Dolls Stickers – sold by Imperial Toys

Chapter 7—The Beauty of Sponsors

Having a company sponsor you is a wonderful thing, especially a company like Pony, Puma or Swatch, JVC and Chams De Baron. Those were some of our sponsors I can recall off the top of my head. I'll tell you, when we would receive one of those large deliveries from our sponsors, it was like Christmas!

Free Pony sneakers, Pumas too, clothing and all the Swatch watches you could ever want. Shoot, I was giving out Swatch watches to my family and friends like crazy. The funny thing? Not any of them has even one of them now. Do you know what those original Swatch watches would be worth today? Buck for sure. I remember we got this Fresh boom box from JVC Electronics that even had a turn table! The guys got that.

A company sponsors you or your crew, band, team, whichever may be the case, and in return you advertise for them. We would wear these products while we performed, especially on live TV or in a movie or commercial. For instance, we (Dynamic) rocked Pony, Puma, Swatch and JVC in our video "The Beat Street Strut."

Also a sponsor will fund a tour, like JVC sponsored a tour we did in the French Antilles for five weeks, paying for everything. So getting a company to sponsor you is very important, and not so easy to do.

I still have my Swatch Watch tee shirt from the 1984 Swatch Watch Fresh Fest tour. What also makes it so special is the art work was done by K. Haring, a famous artist who sadly passed away many years ago. As you can see in the photos, all of the names of the performers on this tour were printed on the back of the shirt.

When we were on "The Morning Show," which was Regis Philbin's talk show one year before Kathy Lee Gifford joined him, we wore these great outfits that were made especially for us by the clothing designer Chams De Baron.

Of course, my outfit had to be pink! Practically everything I wore was pink, did I mention that already? That is why our Puma suits are pink in our video "The Beat Street Strut."

At Chams De Baron Headquarters after our performance live on Regis's "The Morning Show" – June 27, 1984

Kim-A-Kazi (in pink), Susie Q, and JaeCie on the bottom.

Above: The Dolls wearing the official T-shirts from the Swatch Watch Fresh Fest Tour in 1984.

Bottom: Kim-A-Kazi wearing another tour T-shirt, 1984

Chapter 8—Play at Your Own Risk—People Playing Dirty

There is a lot of backstabbing in the entertainment business, and I have certainly seen my share. However, it surprised me sometimes who was actually holding the knife.

Where to start? Well the first thing that comes to mind is an audition for Mountain Dew soda, held at The Roxy in NYC. The Dynamic Dolls and The Dynamic Breakers attended. We were judged as individuals and not as a crew. Two of us were chosen to be in this Mountain Dew commercial, and it was being filmed in Hawaii! When I was younger I had always wanted to go to Hawaii, so I was so excited when I found out they liked me and my crew member Spyder. All I remember is finding out that they had changed their minds and were no longer interested in me.

I didn't understand what happened, until I was informed by several people that this backstabbing bitch Rose, who was a real "wanna be who couldn't be," told the people from Mountain Dew that I was trouble, and they should reconsider because I never showed up on time for anything and that I was very difficult to work with. At least that was the cleaned-up version I got. This backstabbing bimbo was the manager for my boyfriend's crew, The Furious Rockers. She was this scrawny, mousy, doofy white lady who couldn't dance to save her life, never mind break dance. She hid from me for a year and a half.

It is bad enough when other people try to screw you out of opportunities, but what really takes the cake is when the people who are supposed to have your back, who are supposed to get you every opportunity they can, do it to you. Our managers! Now I cannot say for certain that both of my managers did this, but even if one did not sabotage opportunities for The Dolls, she certainly did not do enough for us. When I joined The Dynamic Breakers, they had three managers—two males and a female.

Not long after I signed the contracts, The Dynamic Breakers fired one of the male managers. I do not know why, for I had just gotten there and I had nothing to do with it. In the beginning, Susie and I danced with the guys all the time. It wasn't until sometime later The Dynamic Dolls were created. My manager came up with the name. We were never treated the same as the guys. Our manager put them first, always. You would think if you had the only crew of females that were just as good, if not better, than most male crews out there, that you would take full advantage of the fact that you'd cornered the market.

We also had a female manager, so why she did not take The Dolls and run with it is beyond me. I have even been asked that question during interviews, and all I can think of honestly is Cord, our male manager, did most if not all of the bookings, and she just sat back and collected her fee. Which is why toward the end, it was just Cord managing us. I have my suspicions why Cord did not want The Dolls to overshadow the Dynamic Breakers, but because I do not have solid proof, I will keep my suspicions to myself.

Dynamic's only female manager was Laurita Rock. She has a son, Taimark, who was such a nice guy. I will never forget when he came up to us at The Roxy one day, where we were holding auditions for a music video "Hey DJ" by The World's Famous Supreme Team, who had requested The Dolls to not only be in their video, but to help hold auditions for some other dancers. Taimark was so excited. He told us he had just landed a part in a new movie where he could showcase his martial arts abilities. I remember being so happy for him. Now here is the strange part—not only did we wind up *not* doing the "Hey DJ" video, which for the life of me I can't remember why, but The Dynamic Breakers, our male counterparts, appeared in Taimark's movie "The Last Dragon." Why were The Dynamic Dolls once again left out? As a matter of fact, the guys had cameos in several movies, including "The Exterminator," as well as others. Things that make you go hmmm?

Was this the work of our manager, Cord? It would not be the first or the last career-changing opportunity he would destroy for us.

When we had the deal with Imperial Toys, they made and sold all kinds of products with our name and our pictures on them, such as puffy stickers, wrist and headbands, and shoelaces. They were selling like crazy, so Imperial Toys wanted to make—get this—Dynamic Doll dolls! Yes they wanted to make Barbie dolls that looked just like us. How amazing is that? I found out later that Cord squashed that deal because Imperial only wanted to make dolls from the girls, and not from the guys at that time. Can you blame me for being angry and bitter? I could have had my own Barbie doll, and he ruined that for us. Wait, there is more...

When The Dynamic Breakers were making their record "Total Control," the Dolls were asked to go to Sunshine Records and do the background vocals for the record. We were in the booth doing our "ah ha, ooh hoos" and "That's fresh-fresh" and some other noises, when we had a little break. While the technicians were doing their thing in the control room, we started playing around. I had written a rap for the Dolls and we each had a solo, so we were messing around with the microphone and we started doing out rap. We got so into it that everyone in the control booth stopped what they were doing and listened. Joe Webb, who was the producer, loved it so much that he started recording a record for The Dolls right there on the spot!

Joe Webb gave us a beat, and we started doing our rap. We were almost finished and had recorded the entire record in one take when Cord showed up at the studio. When he walked in and heard the playback of us rapping and saw how excited Joe Webb was about it, he flipped out! Needless to say, he ruined that record. Who knows—maybe we could have gone on to be a successful rap group? Not.

There were many concerts and really good gigs that The Dolls missed out on. I believe we were sent on the lesser gigs, and the guys got the better gigs—for instance, the Pepsi Tour with Michael Jackson! Now why couldn't The

Dolls go on that tour as well? I always wondered, if we would have performed with Michael Jackson on that tour, just where that could have taken The Dolls. That could have led to all kinds of opportunities for us. We may have been in his videos too. Hey, why not—I know several people who were in Michael Jackson's videos.

Even my own partner, Susie Q, had gone off on the sneak and did a couple of gigs without me, including a how-to video, a commercial, and even a quick spot in a movie, "Alphabet City." Now I can go on and on about all of the opportunities that we were screwed out of, but there were a few that I myself walked away from.

One of the biggest gigs I walked away from was the lead role in the movie "Body Rock" with Lorenzo Llamas, and the movie "Beat Street." I did not know I was auditioning for a movie, for real! I was sent to Kronic & Kelly, which was a talent agency that all of The Dynamic Breakers belonged to, so I had to sign up as well. I had been to their office many times, but on this particular day the office was jammed with people.

I was ushered into a waiting room. After my name was taken, I was given a script and told I would be reading the lead female part, and I had to memorize the script for that part. I had never read a script before, but I did what I was told. Nobody told me I had to audition in order to be taken on as a client, but if I had to show I had talent in order to receive representation, then I had to do it.

When they came to get me, I felt I was prepared. There was a lot of cursing in the scene I had to recite, and one part was a long one where I was arguing with my man and there was so much cursing it was difficult to say, like a tongue twister. That was the part I was concerned about. As far as the rest? Hey, I am good at arguing, so no problem. I was brought to this room. It was not very large; it was a square room with a round table in it that barely fit in the room. There were people all around the circular table, and all eyes were on me. I sat down and the lady directly across the table from me began speaking. All I remember at this point in time is she told me she would be running lines with me.

"Whenever you are ready," she told me. "I am ready," I responded.

"*Where is your script?* How are you supposed to read lines with no script?" She was annoyed, as if I was unprepared and wasting their time with my stupidity.

"I was told I had to memorize the part," I told her. Wide-eyed, she looked around at the other people in the room.

"Do you mean to tell me that you have remembered the entire part in such a short amount of time?"

"Yes, I was told I had to," I said. She definitely was impressed, and we began. What is funny about this story is as we were running the lines, I got to that big fight part I was telling you about. I stood up banged my fist on the table, pointed my finger at the lady across from me and very angrily said my lines. That woman jumped out of her seat! It was a good thing I was all the way on the opposite side of the table. If I was any closer, I might have poked her.

They loved me! I received call back after call back, until there were only three of us. They called me in and brought me to a private room set up with a movie camera. They began by asking me some questions, and then told me that they had to decide between me and two other girls for the lead role and that they really wanted to give it to me. However, they needed to ask me one question first. Now you can imagine how I was feeling, I could not imagine what they could possibly have to ask me that was so huge. The funny thing was, I never really got nervous about anything back then. I took everything in stride. Everything was like a new adventure, and I faced it however it came.

"This movie requires partial nudity. Do you have a problem with that?" they asked me.

"I'm sorry, I cannot do that," I answered.

"Well, okay, thank you very much for your time," they said, and then quickly went about their business as if I no longer existed. Not one person looked or spoke to me, so I just left. The actress who got that part owes me a thank you, because if I was one of those people who would do anything to be famous or to have the lead role in a movie, I may have had that part, not her. But I have no regrets. How do you think my husband or my son would feel if their friends came up to them saying, "Hey, man, we just saw your wife/mother all topless in this movie." No thanks. I do however wonder if I had done that movie, if I would have had a career in acting, because I am a very good actress. You do not get picked for the lead role in a movie out of thousands of other actresses unless you have talent, especially with no prior experience. I still plan on trying out my acting skills in the near future. There are just a few things I need to take care of first before I can begin to pursue that dream.

Beat Street the movie. As I have mentioned, The Dynamic Breakers and The Dynamic Dolls were supposed to be in the movie Beat Street, as the rival crew to The Incredible Breakers. Because of several reasons, we backed out, but I was asked if me and the Dolls would still do a few dancing scenes in the movie, and we agreed. I showed up on the day of filming. We were sitting in a school bus and the other Dolls never showed up. I spent over thirteen hours freezing my butt off, and what pissed me off is we spent so much time re-shooting the same scene over and over again.

I guess I couldn't have imagined this movie was going to be the iconic film that it is today. That was *my* mistake.

I also missed out on a chance to be in "Breakin' 2: Electric Boogaloo". Michael (Boogaloo Shrimp) told me that they already had a second movie to Breakin' in the works, and that he wanted me to be in it. I guess it was not meant to be, for every time he called me I was out of the country, and when I returned home and called him back, he was out of the country! We did not have the Internet, cell phones or e-mail back then, so all I could so was leave him a message on his machine.

I found out from Lucinda Dickey's family that casting was done and they had begun filming Electric Boogaloo. The Dolls and I were walking in Times Square, and walking toward us was a group of women. I looked at each one of them, and I knew right away they had to be related to

Lucinda Dickey, for they all looked alike. As we passed, they looked at me and I looked at them, and we turned around to face one another. I find it very funny that her own family saw such a resemblance in me to their sister. Even her mother was amused, and they all said, "Oh my God, you look like Lucinda." Now other than being a white female with short dark hair, I do not see it, but it must be true and here is why...

It was 1984 in New York City, and Dynamic received a special invitation to the premiere showing of a new break dancing movie from the west coast called "Breakin'." I remember standing in the front of the line, and a door opened and out came the two lead actors of the movie, Shabba Doo and Boogaloo Shrimp. Immediately Shrimp and I recognized one another from the first time we met at the Fun House. I'll never forget it. I was standing on the back stage, which was the Hip Hop stage, and I looked over at the big stage where the shows were put on. This stage was known as the "Buggers'" stage where mostly the white boys danced, so it was weird to see this guy up on the Buggers' stage popping.

I watched him, and he was good, I liked his style—it was sharp. He spotted me and we faced each other from across the club. He threw out a few moves, and I copied them back. I will never forget the look on his face, shocked to see a white girl who was that skilled. Anyway, we threw a few moves back and forth for a while, and then I waved him over. "You belong back here with us," I told him. Anyway, that is how we first met.

So now we were at the premiere in New York City for the movie "Breakin'" and Shrimp and Shabba Doo were addressing the crowd by saying a few words and showing off a few dance moves. It was time to go inside, and the doors opened. All of a sudden I was being whisked away by these big guys, which I soon realized were hired bodyguards for Shrimp and Shabba Doo—only they were pulling me along with them. The next thing I knew, I was seated in a back row on the aisle seat right next to Shrimp, Shabba Doo, their manager, and everyone else who was associated with the movie. It soon became clear to me that I was being mistaken for Lucinda Dickey by the bodyguards! How funny is that?

So there I was, sitting among the stars of the film, and I see my crew walking down the aisle looking back with confusion, like "What the heck is Kim-A-Kazi doing sitting over there near the stars?" It really was very funny. Afterward I was invited back to the hotel for an after-party. Brenda K Starr had gone with me. I do not really remember too much of that party, except I had made plans with Shrimp and his manager (a very lovely lady) to return the next day before they had to go to the airport to take them shopping in the Village. I returned the next day and we took their limo to the Village, where the guys purchased a bunch of items, including spiked wrist bands and neck pieces. I was glad I got to show them a small piece of New York on their visit.

Michael "Boogaloo Shrimp" tells me he will never forget we were standing in the lobby of the hotel, discussing—what else? dancing—and he said he remembers I dropped to the floor and began breaking. I was showing him a few East Coast moves, but if you are a dancer, you will not find anything strange about what I did. Just think of all the strange places you just busted out and started dancing. On the subways, subway platforms, airports. I think whenever we stood still for more than a few minutes we automatically started dancing, no matter where we were.

We had kept in touch for a while and then lost touch. I am happy to say I reunited with both men. Shabba Doo was doing a show out here in Las Vegas where we live, so my husband I met Shabba Doo at his hotel, where we all had breakfast before he headed back to California. We had a great time. I usually do not get up that early in the morning for too many people. I have not been able to see Michael "Boogaloo Shrimp" face to face yet, but we finally found one another and keep in touch. And more recently, I was a guest on Shabba-Doo's radio spot called "Breakin' News."

Shabba Doo and Kim-A-Kazi in Las Vegas 2010

Let's go back to the video with World's Famous Supreme Team called "Hey DJ Won't You Play That Song" in 1984.

We held the auditions at The Roxy, and while we were going over the lyrics, the dancers were warming up for the auditions. This was when I met my son's father. He was with the Coney Island crew "The Furious Rockers." Needless to say, they are in the video—along with that snake in the grass manager of theirs who had screwed up the Mountain Dew commercial for me. She is the scrawny, unattractive old white lady with no skills or rhythm in the video. Can you say "hate?" I am sorry, but when you purposely set out to ruin somebody else's chances at a great opportunity that they had worked very hard for, just because you do not have the talent or the skills to honestly get the job, I find that disgraceful and evil. I worked so very hard to reach the level of skills that I had. I have a real problem with people who try to take shortcuts.

Mr. Speed, president of The Furious, told me that his manager Roseanne was a terrible manager. He said she got greedy and started taking more of their money for herself, and then she started riding their coattails and began auditioning herself for the same gigs they were. We had picked The Furious Rockers as one of the crews to appear in the "Hey DJ" video, and as you can see when watching it, he wasn't lying about his manager, because she worked her way into that video although she has no skills. A manager is usually not in the habit of using their clients to try and get gigs themselves. Most managers are happy to let their clients do the gig, and they just collect their share of the paycheck.

Me and every B-Girl and B-Boy out there who are at the top of their game have worked long and hard. Just because we may make it look easy, it goes to show how hard we worked. Nothing about break dancing is easy, especially for females. We do not have the same upper body strength that guys do. I am not saying we are not as strong; I think we have proved that we are. What I am saying is that guys naturally have more upper body strength than women, just as most women have stronger leg muscles than most guys. We are built differently for a reason.

I believe that B-Girls are more accepted by B-Boys today than they were back in my time. I believe guys are more willing to teach girls how to break or pop because we are now seen as an asset to a crew. I am not saying that our guys were not supportive. They were, but it was not like they took us aside and showed us step by step how to do moves such as windmills or head spins. I must give a lot of credit to my Dolls, because they were not afraid to get down on the floor and get hurt.

Susie had to trust me explicitly when I put her on my head and let go with my hands to spin her. Susie had to do her part too—she had great ab muscles, which helped her to stay up there. I am proud to say I have never dropped anyone when spinning them, and I say this with pride because I know many other guys who have dropped people when doing the 3-man or the helicopter.

Chapter 9—Wild and Crazy Times

In life we all have our good times and our bad times. However, when you are a performer you cannot afford to have a bad performance, and I must say we always gave our absolute best when we walked out on that stage. There are a few exceptions. It was during that long tour to the French Antilles that I mentioned in chapter three, when we were thrown out of that radio station. Well, we were invited to this formal restaurant which also had a nightclub. It was kind of like its own area. Picture a room with two entrances directly across from one another. To get through this room, you had to walk straight through across the dance floor and out the other door, which led back into the restaurant. On either sides of the dance floor there were these carpeted levels, almost like bleachers, to sit on and watch people dance.

We had no intentions of doing anything that evening but relaxing while enjoying a nice dinner and the night off. My manager had this little habit of offering free performances to people, and this is what he did that evening. Now, I do not know if they offered to comp our meal or what, but Cord informed us after we ate that we would be putting on a little show. The Fresh Kids refused, so it was up to Susie Q and me. Now we had just finished eating a large meal, and the last thing we wanted to do was break dance for free. We were good sports and obliged them. The announcement was made, and in the blink of an eye there was a large crowd already packed into the room I described.

Susie and I began doing a routine and the crowd was loving it, begging for more. There was this part of the routine where Susie Q and I separated to opposite sides of the floor, and after a small routine apart, she would run toward me and up she would go, into the air, where I would hold her above my head with one arm. Then after I spun around a few times, I would drop her down onto my head and do the helicopter where I spin Susie Q on my head—but that did not happen.

What did happen was, while Susie Q and I had separated and were doing our routine apart, I saw her laughing. Knowing her as well as I do, I knew exactly what was going on. Susie Q was letting them rip—she had gas. Whenever we were in a club and Susie Q was dancing, she usually had a circle around her, but when I saw a circle with nobody in it, I knew it was the work of Susie Q. She would fart so badly that it had a Moses effect and separated the crowd! I swear. Well, this was exactly what she was doing now, in the middle of our performance. She was really laughing hard, and I saw the people sitting closest to her start to move away with that look of disgust on their faces. I guess "phew" is the same in any language!

Now Susie was supposed to run toward me to gain some momentum so I could lift her clear over my head, but she didn't do that either. Because we were so tired from this long tour, and we were now laughing so hard we were unable to execute these moves. Instead of running to me, Susie was hysterically laughing, heading toward me like a drunk trying to run up a hill. She finally made her way across the dance floor to me, but instead of jumping up to help me lift her, she just stood there shaking from laughter. Laughing myself, I managed to lift her up, but not over my head into the air like I was supposed to.

Instead I picked her dead weight up and placed her on my head. Susie was usually straight as an arrow when I placed her on my head, as you can see in the photos, but she was now hanging there like a wet noodle on top of my head. I was trying to spin her so the force would straighten her out, but I couldn't. I cannot remember too much after that, except that Cord was pissed off at us and the Fresh Kids were laughing their asses off. Cord later forgave us because he knew we were exhausted, and he did spring that performance on us with no warning.

Another disastrous performance coincidently occurred on the same tour, except this one was in Guyana. We were about to do this performance at one of those outdoor arenas where the stage is shaped like a huge oyster shell. The crowd was massive, and I do not know why, but instead of entering the stage from backstage as we always would, we had to fight our way through the crowd to get to the stage. We formed a single file line and tried to navigate through the crowd. As I was walking though the sea of people, I felt someone not just grab my butt, they palmed my left cheek and tested it, like someone squeezing a cantaloupe to see if it is firm.

Now when I was in school, the boys used to run by me and try to grab my butt. They knew they needed a running start because I had developed a reflex of punching whoever had grabbed me from behind. That was how often it happened. I do not know what was so irresistible about my butt that guys were compelled to grab it, but they did. Even my husband says it was one of the first things he noticed about me. Gee, thanks, honey.

So there I was, minding my own business, when someone palmed my butt. My immediate reaction was to turn and hit, so I turned with my right fist cocked and I paused. This guy who stood about 6'1 was standing there with a big old grin on his face, which to me added insult to injury. So I let my right go and punched him dead in his jaw! His smile immediately disappeared as his eyes rolled back into his head and he keeled over. He looked just like one of those big, tall trees when they get chopped down and the lumberjack yells "Timber!" and the tree just falls over. That is just what he looked like. His friends caught him, and as I turned to continue on my way, one of the Fresh Kids—I do not remember which one—was wide-eyed, as if he could not believe what had just happened. He just looked at me and we continued onto the stage.

That one incident started a full-out riot! We were on stage, and I don't think we got through half of our performance when bottles, rocks and other objects were being hurled at the stage, at us. That was it—we were out of there. We left the stage and headed out to our bus. We would have been out of there then, but one of the guys had disappeared and we could not leave without him. The crowd had now spilled out into the parking lot and surrounded our bus.

We showed no fear, and as they attacked the bus trying to get to us, I was hanging out of a window punching and shoving people off the bus. Then finally the missing guy showed up, and how he got through that angry mob and onto the bus alive is a mystery to me. The mob began to rock the bus when finally the driver took off. Man, that was one crazy situation. We had never had a negative situation from any audience before. I got hassled at times, though.

It seemed to happen the most while I was on the Swatch Watch Fresh Fest Tour. Sometimes I would come out from the dressing rooms and walk into the arena to peek at some of the performances, like Run DMC or Kurtis Blow. I was not visible to the audience unless they looked down over the railing. This was also the place that we waited while the MC announced us before running onto the center stage. No matter which time I was standing there, I would usually hear the same taunts. "Shoo what's that white girl doing here? What's she gonna do?" was one comment I mostly got.

Anyway, they would make their comments until they actually saw me perform. As I exited the arena, those same females were now whooping and hollering for me, yelling "yeah, you go, girl." It was one of those times that prompted me to pick up Buffy from The Fat Boys.

On this particular night, there was a large group of females that had come to see the show. When they spotted me waiting for our turn to take the stage, I received the usually nasty remarks—only this time it was worse, for there were so many of them and they seemed to fuel each other's hatred for me. During my performance, every move was on point, and I seemed to just rock every move more than usual. I was so pumped when I came off the stage and saw the entire group of females screaming and cheering for me.

As I stated, I was so pumped that I went to pick up someone and Buffy was right there. I think there was a fleeting moment when my brain said "are you fucking crazy?" but to me, it just made my victory greater. I got behind Buffy and attempted to pick him up. My first try failed, for I could not get my arms around his belly! So I had to go under his belly and find his waist. I clasped my hands and up he went! I spun him around several times to the gasps of the people around us. I think Buffy himself was somewhat shocked.

Even my own brother-in-law did not really believe that I had picked up one of The Fat Boys, even though he knew I was very strong. So one day he ran into The Fat Boys at a car dealership in Brooklyn, and he asked them.

"Do you know my sister-in-law Kim from The Dynamic Dolls?" he asked. When they confirmed that they knew me, he asked if I really picked up Buffy and spun him around. Of course they said, "Hells yeah." I remember every time I went to Tin Pan Apple to see their manager, Charles Stettler, Charles would tell the entire office, "You see this girl? She picked up Buffy—she actually picked up Buffy." I am sure that didn't help my already crumpling body. As they say, "Pride cometh before a fall."

One of my biggest injuries that affected my dancing abilities the most occurred on my home turf, The Roxy. It is not my worst injury, medically speaking, but it was the injury that put an end to most of my break dancing moves. We were hired to do a show for Liza Minnelli and Chita Rivera to celebrate the opening night of their new Broadway show called "The Rink." It was a real honor to be selected as the entertainment for the evening's event. As you can imagine, all of Hollywood's finest were there, such as Bernadette Peters and Lucille Ball!

I used to manage this high-end cosmetics boutique, the job I quit to pursue my dancing career. I swear, just about every single day someone would tell me, "You know who you look like?" The answer was always the same: "Bernadette Peters." And I do mean every single day. So when I met Bernadette Peters that night, I shared this information with her.

Bernadette Peters turned to the man she was with and gave him a knowing look. I apologized and told her I hoped I did not offend her.

"No!, Not at all," she assured me. "It's just that I get so many people who come up to me and say, *'Oh, everyone tells me I look just like you,'* and I would turn to my husband and ask, *'Oh my God is that what I really look like?'*"

She assured me that in my case, it was a real compliment. I was like, "Whew." To be told you are so unattractive that a celebrity was insulted at the thought of being compared to looking like you is a real deep insult.

I had asked the maintenance guy from The Roxy to make sure they did not wax the floor for that evening's event, and if he had to wax or polish the wooden floors, to not do the area where we were to perform. That request went unfulfilled. Everything was great until the finale. I had choreographed it to end with every one of us spinning. Some of the guys were doing windmills, Duce was doing head spins and Susie Q was doing floats, and I was doing hand glides. However, they had waxed the floor after all, and I had a 'do-rag over my hand to help me spin faster— and faster I did spin! I spun so fast that I twisted my entire wrist. Thank goodness it was at the very end of the performance.

What happened next was pretty cool. Liza Minnelli and Chita Rivera were sitting a few feet away from me at a table with a bucket with champagne in it. They removed the bottle of champagne from the bucket of ice and put my hand in it. My hand was extremely swollen, red, and it hurt. Someone had gotten me a bandage and wrapped my left arm, wrist and hand in it. All I really remember after that was walking around The Roxy enjoying myself.

The Roxy had been turned into a carnival with game booths where you could win prizes, just like a real carnival. I was able to win a few, mostly because I am right-handed. However, my left hand was the hand I used to do hand glides, windmills and lift people up in the air before lowering them onto my head. After that night I could no longer do any of those things, and I was pissed! I had just got my windmills down and was working on the speed, so I never really got to show them off. I believe if you do not have a move or a trick down, then you should not show it in public until you have perfected it. I could not respect myself if I did slow or sloppy windmills, or any move for that matter, especially in a performance.

Between the torn rotator cuff and the torn ligaments in my left shoulder and arm, I could not use my left arm, wrist or hand in any physical capacity. Even years later, I went to take boxing classes just to keep in shape and I was asked to do some pull-ups and chin-ups. I got up on the high bar and could not even hang from it, nonetheless do pull-ups! I also started training "south paw" because I could not hold my left up to constantly jab, so my right became my jab hand and my left my power punch.

Today I still have the damage in my left wrist, and because I didn't know I had a torn rotator cuff in my left shoulder, it was never treated and I developed bursitis, tendonitis and arthritis from my left hand all the way up my arm to my neck and down my back. Not to mention carpal tunnel in both hands. My advice to *you* is to take as many protective steps as you can while practicing and learning a new move or skill, and if you do get hurt, go get it checked by a doctor. If you do what I did and ignore your injuries and continue to perform, you will make it worse, and you will have pain for the rest of your life. So *don't do it.*

Another crazy event happened after we had done a special appearance at a club in Canada named Club Soda. I love that name. All I can remember about that trip was, our performance was outstanding, so much so that I was deemed the Best Female Break Dancer in the Country. Terry Tuff was the DJ that night. We had to leave for the airport early the next morning for the guys—yes, the guys had a show to do at The New York Coliseum in Manhattan, where the New York Men's Wear Show was being held. I do not know what had transpired that night, because as usual I was alone in my room. However, one of our crew members had not come down to the hotel lobby, and we were ready to leave for the airport. We called his room repeatedly, and then a few of the guys went up and banged on his door. Nothing! Finally we had to call the hotel manager and ask him to please open the door, so we could make sure he was okay.

The manager went up to the room and tried to open the door, but the inside bolt was engaged. I don't know why they did not cut the chain, but they screamed through the door and this guy still did not wake up! They could hear him snoring, so they knew he was okay. I think he had managed to take the phone off the hook, because the line was busy. We had no choice but to leave him there. This dead-to-the-world sleeper was Spyder, and yes, we went to the airport and left Spyder in Canada.

Once again I had to come to the rescue and be the fifth performer in the show. The best part was, I got some really great leather to keep. I got the white leather driving gloves that were like butter. I remember we all got some leather apparel, shorts or pants, and the guys got leather shirts too. I was happy with my leather driving gloves, which I am wearing in one of the earlier photographs in this book.

As for Spyder, he finally woke up and realized we had left without him, I know he was not happy, but what were we to do? We could have all stayed behind, but what good would have come from that? We would have missed our performance at the Men's Show, and they could have sued us. It was Spider's fault for staying out late, and for taking the phone off the hook and putting the bolt on his door so even management could not gain entry.

Just my luck: We were lucky enough to have been requested to perform alongside the amazing Chaka Khan at the Beacon Theatre in Manhattan for the entire weekend. I have just a few memories—such as while performing, I'd just finished spinning someone on my head and Chaka Khan was standing just to my left. I turned, and she looked at me right in my eyes and mouthed "Wow" to me, and then gave me a big smile. She was electrifying! She gave off her own energy—and forget about that voice! It was a fun show.

It was a rarity, but the following week I found myself home without any obligations. A day off. I was at my mom's house and I was hanging out in my sister's room, listening to the stereo. 92 WKTU was the original station when I heard they were giving away a great prize to the 92nd caller. I did not hear what they were giving away, but I started dialing anyway.

Now for you young people, keep in mind this was 1983 or '84. We did not have speed dial or re-dial, and many people still owned rotary phones. We had no computers, no cell phones—heck, we didn't even have beepers yet. So you can just imagine how hard it was to dial in and win. But I won! I was the 92nd caller. And do you know what they were giving away? Yep, I won tickets to see Chaka Khan in concert at the Beacon Theatre! I told the host to give them away to another caller, because I had just performed with Chaka Khan at the Beacon Theatre. I think the only prize that could have topped that was winning tickets to watch myself perform at one of our shows, But I thought that was a funny story, because that is Just My Luck.

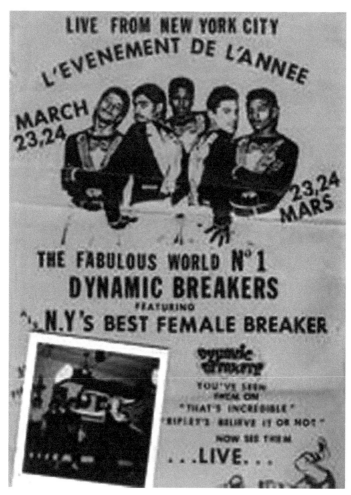

Kim-A-Kazi joins the guys in Canada—where I was named "Best Female Breaker in the Country"

Italy

If I didn't have enough to deal with, I now had to deal with a group of immature boys. On one of our trips to Italy, it was not just us—we had an entire entourage of talent. Rappers, graffiti artists, and other dancers. This was a unique show; it was a non-stop performance. I'll never forget the beautiful hotel we were staying at. It was a real castle perched high upon a mountain, and its architecture was stunning, not to mention the surrounding scenery.

Because there were so many of us, we had occupied several rooms. Some rooms had more than one bedroom, and some, like Susie's and mine, had a sitting room, then a bedroom with two twin beds, a balcony, and a bathroom. One night Kano, who was Susie Q's fiancé and later her husband, was not feeling well, so she went to his room to take care of him. Because he and Airborne shared the same style room as we had, there were just two twin beds, so Airborne had come to stay with me in my room while Susie remained with Kano.

Now there were times the girls had to share a room with the guys before, and we were treated with respect. They were like our brothers. They protected us when we had to change backstage by surrounding us with a sheet (sometimes the dressing rooms are too far from the stage—most performers know how this goes).

Well, no sooner had we retired into our own separate beds and were falling asleep when our telephone started ringing. Groggily I answered it, and I heard juvenile panting and sex noises coming from the other end. Listen, I am no stranger to pranks. The Dynamic Breakers are some of the funniest guys I have ever had the privilege of knowing. But this was not funny—it was annoying and insulting to me.

After the second childish phone call, I took the phone off the hook. Then they started ringing our doorbell. Each room had a doorbell, because the doors were so thick and made of solid carved wood that knocking could not always be heard. They continued to ring the bell and make stupid suggestions outside our door. You could hear them laughing while running back down the hall to their room.

I was so tired, and since Airborne was out like a light, it was up to me to put an end to this. So when they saw I was not coming to the door, they got a little braver and did not run back to their room so quickly. I waited until they were just outside my door, I quietly went to the door, and as they were planning their next attack, I ripped open the door and snarled like a wild animal.

Well, they went running and screaming down the hallway, and while they were all trying to get into their room at the same time, they became jammed up at the doorway. They tried to climb over one another to get inside. They made it inside and slammed the door and locked it, all the while laughing at their escape. Well, I was fired up and gave this door a side kick. It made this cracking noise, and when I kicked it again something split. It was apparent that I could kick this solid door in, so they unlocked it and ran for cover in the other rooms.

I was after the ring leader, Chico, and he knew it. He ran into the bedroom and bolted the door. Boom! I busted the door open with one kick, ripping the bolt from the door frame. The coward dove under the bed, pleading with me and apologizing over and over again. I warned him that if he did anything else to me, he was going to be very sorry. As I left their room and headed back to mine I could hear them come up with a new nickname for me: "She Man." It took me a little while to make them stop calling me that, for I did not like it. So they just called me Hercules, emphasis on the *Her*. Silly boys.

Castle we stayed at in Italy while on tour

The narrow streets of Italy. People had packed the streets and were hanging off of their balconies when we arrived. (You can see the crowd in the photo on page 100)

The only other event I can recall from that trip happened during the performance. It was a fair sized audience, and the stage was about seven feet off the ground. During some of our performances, we like to come off of the stage and into the audience, sometimes dancing with them. We did just that during this performance. I remember a little old man a few rows back and several seats in from the aisle. He was having such a good time dancing and he looked anxious for me to come and say hi, so I did. In his excitement, the older man grabbed me, hugged me and pinched my cheeks, saying "Bella, Bella." Before we knew what was happening, the security guards came running down the aisle and grabbed the old man, ready to throw him out of the show. "No, No," I protested, and let them know it was okay and they should not touch the old man. They finally left him alone, and he showed his gratitude by once again pinching my cheeks and saying, "Bella."

I was glad that was settled. By now I could hear my crew members yelling my name and waving me back to the stage. Our routine was just about to begin again, and I had but seconds to make my way back to the front and up onto the stage. I ran down the aisle and jumped! My fingertips reached the top of the stage, and I tried to pull myself up but I could not, to my surprise. I pulled with all my strength, but with just my fingertips holding on, I could not get up there. With my legs dangling above the floor below, I had nothing to help me get up from this awkward position. Finally two of the guys came to the edge of the stage and helped pull me up, just in time for me to fall into line and begin our routine. Whew!

I think the story of when we first arrived in Italy should make this chapter. You need to understand that we had no idea that anyone in this faraway place could possibly know about us, so it was my suggestion that we change that. We took our boom box and some flyers for the show, and we headed out. We found this quaint little park with cobble stone streets and some grass and benches. We figured it would be a perfect place to do a little routine and pass out the flyers to the crowd. This way, maybe some people would come to our show.

So we turned on the music and we started dancing. Well, before you could do a 1990, there was a huge crowd surrounding us, People everywhere. All of a sudden, I saw what looked like the military! They were in uniforms and they had these weapons over their shoulders and ammunition across their chests. *Oh my God!* I thought, *we are going to jail, or worse!*

Our translator pulled me aside and told me to climb the steps—there was a statue in the park that had steps leading up to the statue perched atop. As I climbed the steps and was head and shoulders above everyone else, I could not believe my eyes! There were people as far as the eye could see. And if that wasn't amazing enough, people were hanging off their balconies! What we obviously did not know was not only had these people known who we were, they had been anticipating our arrival. As you can imagine, it got pretty crazy after that.

The police wanted to whisk us away, but we convinced them to let us go through the crowds and stop every so often to do a little performance for the people. So we did. I only have one photo left of this event, but in the ones I no longer have, you could see everything I am telling you. Once we had reached our tour bus, we were heading back to our hotel. We decided we should not attempt to do this again. As the bus drove away, we had a few dozen people give chase on their mopeds. Most people drive these little scooters around over there, for the streets can be narrow.

Occasionally the hotel security could not keep all the fans out, and some of them would make their way to our rooms. How they knew what rooms we were in is a mystery to me. All I do know is they always seemed to come to our room first—the girls' room. We were always accommodating, signing a few autographs, but they wanted more. I don't know if they wanted us to invite them in or what, but we always got rid of them by telling them which room the guys were in.

I must admit, our second tour to Italy was much better, and it was only Dynamic on the trip so it was very enjoyable. As a matter of fact, the guys were so funny, charming and flirty with the flight attendants that they got us all bumped up to first class! First class on an eleven-hour flight is a real pleasure. We had a stopover in Rome on the way to the Island of Sardinia. However, the airlines were on strike and we would end up getting stuck in the airport in Rome, Italy, for just about twenty-four hours! So what did we do? Of course, we made the best of it, and occasionally we would dance.

Without the intention of doing so, we actually made quite a bit of money from people coming over and watching us and giving us money. We finally had to put out a hat or a cup to collect the money in. We were just doing what most dancers do, especially when they are bored or standing still too long—we danced. As I mentioned earlier, I would get bored on the train, or waiting on the platform for the train or subway, and I would dance. I didn't blow out full routines or anything, but I would try out new moves or practice my skills, and sometimes just move for fun.

We never really danced in the streets for money. However, one day we were walking down 34th Street in Manhattan, and me and the girls heard loud music coming from down the block near Madison Square Garden. We saw some guys we knew who had just been in our video, "The Beat Street Strut." We went over to mess with them. We used to always kid around with one another. The leader of the crew's name was "Klown," and he was definitely a clown. Anyway, we started giving them a hard time about breaking on the street for money, and they started talking all kinds of crap about how they could make more money than we could. So I said, "Put your money where your big mouth is." We made a bet that The Dynamic Dolls could break dance for just a few minutes, and we would make more than they did all day long. They took that bet.

Now, they already had a small circle of spectators standing around, but not many. No sooner did we take our places in the circle, than me, Susie Q and JaeCie had a bunch of new people flock around us. And we didn't even do anything yet! The music started and we did our thing. After about five minutes, we took our bows, and people weren't even waiting for the hat to be passed around. They had been putting money in the hat since we started. And there were every denomination of bills, up to twenties, so when the people had finished giving the money, I put my hand in the hat and took a fistful, and we said "thanks" and left. Whatever I took from their hat was not even half. We did leave them the lion's share, so it was a win-win situation.

Please do not misunderstand; I have nothing against street performing at all. It's just that we were fortunate enough to have so much work, we did not have to. I like that break dancing gave many kids an opportunity they did not have before, a chance to make money for themselves and for their families.

OLBIA SARDEGNA, ITALY
MUSIC & DANCE FESTIVAL '84
UN'ISCOLA SARDA SAFERULA
FEB. 23, 1984

Susie Q & Duce –Up rock Battle in Italy–Kano, Kim-A-Kazi, Cord in the crowd, lower right. Notice the police holding back the crowds

I was not a bully or a showoff. Oh, don't get me wrong—when it came time to perform, I gave my all. When I was in a battle I did my thing, but what I am talking about is always trying to be the center of attention, always trying to steal the spotlight. If there was another female at the club in a circle and she was popping, sometimes my friend would be like, "Yo, Kim, go in and take her. She sucks." Why? Because I can?

If she wasn't bothering me, then let her do her thing. So what? I knew I was better than her. I didn't have to prove it constantly. Let her have her time in the spotlight; let her do her thing. I had a friend who was like that. If she saw someone dancing and they were good, she would have to run over there and try to out-dance them. And the funny thing was, this girl was not that good to begin with. I dance when I hear music that I like, music that moves me. I never got on a dance floor out of jealousy or spite.

This so-called friend tried that shit on me once! Before I tell you this particular story, let me give you a little background. The first time I met this girl, she was dancing and she had some chip on her shoulder. I had given her a compliment on her looks and she got all defensive. Her friend told me not to pay her any mind, because she had a complex. When I took another look, I could see why, and I found out later she was teased for her looks. So dancing was really her only way of receiving attention—and if someone else was better than her, oh boy! I remember the first time she turned on me because of dancing.

She had begged me over and over again to join up with the dancing school she was going to. She wanted us to take these two classes' together, tap and jazz. Finally I agreed, and she picked me up at my house and we would go together. These classes were intermediate classes, which meant they were in between beginner and advanced classes.

Now my friend had been taking these classes for some time, and when I joined the class it had started several weeks earlier, which meant I had to play catch-up. Other than the few lessons I joined in when I was nine, I had never been to a dance class before, but I took to it like a fish to water and she did not like that. Not only did I catch up to the rest of the class in both jazz and tap, but I began to excel. She did not like that either.

What really put the last straw on her back was when the teacher started using me as an example to the rest of the class, especially when it came to spins and turns—my specialty. The teacher would ask me to come to the front of the classroom and demonstrate the proper way to do the move. Now, I could see her being upset if I pranced around like Miss Thang or if I was taking bows up there, but I was not.

To make a long and childish story shorter, she stopped picking me up so we could walk to class together, and after class was over she took off without me. Finally I said "to hell with this." I only joined to begin with because of her, so if this was going to ruin our friendship, then I may as well quit. So I did. This was the first of several displays of jealousy, and although they extended to other things like friends and boyfriends, I will only speak of the ones pertaining to dancing.

The next problem came when she started coming with me to The Fun House. I was already an original member of The Juice Crew. The Juice Crew was formed because a bunch of people who loved to dance started hanging out together every weekend at The Fun House. Well, one of the unofficial leaders of our crew had gotten us a gig, but because The Juice Crew had so many dancers in it, there was no way we could all be in the show.

The same unofficial leaders of our crew picked the best dancers out of all of us, and they would perform and represent the rest of our crew. I believe there were only five dancers picked to perform, and I was one of them. Guess who was not? Can you hear another wedge being driven between us? Mama Juice was also not chosen to be in the show, so those two became as thick as thieves. Hey, it wasn't my fault that they were not chosen.

I will never forget the first time I saw a crew called The Floor Masters, A.K.A. Rockers Revenge/Incredible Breakers at The Fun House. These boys were amazing! I mentioned them earlier when I broke my collarbone. Anyway, brothers Chino, Brian and Sammy, along with their crew members, took the House by storm! One of their crew members began popping, and I was not only amazed at his skills, but I was hooked. That guy was known as Mike Boogie. It is because of that guy that I really began popping.

That night I was sleeping over at my friend's house, and the next morning as soon as I opened my eyes, I thought of that guy popping. I jumped right out of bed and stood in front of the mirror. I remembered how it looked, and I began breaking down my body. I started with my right hand, first the tips of my fingers, then the knuckles, wrist, elbow, shoulder, and then onto the left side. It did not take me long at all to learn the moves, and I was so excited I turned to my friend and said, "Come on, come learn with me so we can do it together." But she was not interested. She was one of those girls that if it did not look sexy, she wasn't interested. Oh, well. I continued teaching myself, and I even choreographed a little popping routine.

My Popping Debut

About two weeks later, we were at our turf (The Back Stage) at The Fun House and Jellybean played the song I had been practicing my little popping routine to. I was excited to show all my friends what I had learned, and it did not take long to finish my routine, for as a beginner who was learning by herself, I didn't have many moves. All of a sudden, a big commotion was going on somewhere behind me. People were yelling and there was thunderous applause. As much as I wanted to hear what my friends thought of my popping routine, I had to turn around to see what was going on. They were clapping for me! I could not believe it, I was stunned, and I'll tell you why.

Where my friends and I were was kind of like a cozy corner, and with it being somewhat dark at times, depending on the lights and the pattern they were flashing, you don't really think anyone can really see you—not to mention hundreds of other people in the club. So I figured Michael Jackson or someone big walked in (he did one night, but that's a different story). So I turned around and all these people, and even the people on the second floor, were all clapping for me, and someone yelled out, *"Do more, Do more."*

I said, "I can't. That's all I know how to do."

"Do it again. Do it again," they shouted back at me.

I stood there for a moment, thinking to myself, "Once I do this again, they are going to realize I am not all that." I hoped they would not boo me this time. So I took a deep breath and thought very carefully about each move, so I did not mess it up. You have to keep in mind that I had only just begun to learn how to do this form of dance, where you need to be in touch with every part of your body. Every single muscle and joint, and you had to control them one by one, yet make them look fluid at the same time.

When I was done, I was met with the same enthusiasm that they had cheered me on with the first time. That was not only a great feeling, but it gave me the confidence to continue learning how to pop. I can say with certainty, and as modestly as I possibly can, that I was the best female popper of my day, and there were only a handful of guys who could really take me. All right, maybe two handfuls, because there were some skilled people back then. I never really bothered to learn how to "lock," mostly because it just did not look right on me. However, I did put a few small locking moves into a routine I choreographed for me and Susie Q.

Needless to say, once I started getting all of this attention for my popping abilities, guess who wanted to learn how to pop all of a sudden? Come on, I bet you'll never guess. That's right! She wanted the attention and I tried to teach her, but she just wasn't any good at it, and I do not think she was willing to practice day and night to get better. One straw to go.

One night at The Roxy, I along with the other Dolls, Susie Q and JaeCie, were enjoying a night out surrounded by our many friends. I was off on my own, dancing and enjoying these dancers who took turns showing off their moves in a circle, when the girls came over to me, not looking very happy. I asked them what was wrong, and they complained that "your friends" were dancing all up in their faces, trying to battle them—challenge them—and the girls did not like it. "Oh please," I told them, "why are you even wasting your time? They aren't even a real break dance crew. They are jazz dancers." So that seemed to appease the girls, and they went on their way.

Not long after that, the girls returned to where I was, even angrier. "Yo, they're doing it again. Let's go battle them," JaeCie said.

"Come on, we are not wasting our time," I said again. "There is no competition. They are Solid Gold wannabes." The girls hung out with me after that when all of a sudden, who comes over to me but two of my ex-Juice Crew members and their girls. Edna and the other girl came over to me, making all nice and friendly.

"We're doing a show at this place, and then another one at this place," they were bragging. Meanwhile the places they claimed to be dancing at were tiny little hole-in-the-wall places in Brooklyn, New York. "So what are you doing?" they asked in a smug way.

Well, after I announced several huge events including a live national television show and a tour and a h,ost of other gigs anyone would love to do, they did not look so smug any longer. What they did next blew my mind!

At first they just looked as though they were dancing, having a good time, but it quickly became apparent that these fools were trying to battle *me*! My girls were standing there with their arms folded, with these big smiles on their faces.

"What's the matter, Kim? You don't like it, huh?" they said. And they were right I did not like it, and now I knew how my girls felt when it was done to them. All excited and ready to take them on, I called my girls over to the side. "They want to battle, right? Well, we are going to do this Dynamic style."

I then went up to the deejay booth and I asked Richie the house D.J., "Hey Richie, you want a free show?" He was like, "Hell yeah, what's up?" I briefed him on the situation and I asked him to play a certain song for us. Well, he stopped the music and announced that we, "The Famous Dynamic Dolls," were going to give a performance that evening. Richie went all out with spotlights, and he even dropped the large screen behind the stage that we were going to perform on, and ran our video "The Beat Street Strut" while we rocked that place.

While we were performing, I watched those Solid Gold wannabes walk out of the club. After the show was over, I told my girls, "Now that's how we do it Dynamic style." Sorry, but they asked for it!

Note: Years later, I had reconnected with those two girls from the other crew because of a mutual friend. However, because of Edna's constant jealousy, sabotage and lies, I severed that relationship for good. If there is anyone in your life who has a negative effect on you, you should cut them out of your life and only surround yourself with good, positive people.

I was speaking to a friend of mine who is making a documentary unlike any other, and it is all about a magical place you have heard me mention time and time again in my book.

The documentary is about The Fun House. You have heard it here that I predict this film will be extremely successful. Nick, the man who is making this masterpiece, is an amazing person who has worked long and hard on his documentary. I, for one, cannot wait to see it.

Now I have had conversations with a lot of people in the past few years that I have not seen or spoken to in almost twenty-five years or more. And in this industry, there are some with enormous egos. The way some people tell it, you would think that it was them and only them that created break dancing, popping, locking, and Hip Hop itself. When I speak to Nick, he is always talking about other dancers and graciously gives so many people props. He, like me, enjoys watching other people dance, especially when they are good and enjoying themselves. After all, that is what dancing is all about—enjoying one's self and self-expression.

Chapter 10—Battle, Anyone?

As we progressed in our careers, we did not really battle any longer. First of all, we were too busy always traveling on tour and working; and secondly, there really wasn't anyone to battle. I am not trying to sound conceited, but there wasn't.

As a Dynamic Doll it was even worse, because there just were not any females to battle us, and even though we did have a few brave B-Boy crews who felt up to the challenge, there wasn't really any competition. I had more battle as just Kim-A-Kazi as a popper than as a Dynamic Doll, and that was always against guys. I had one battle with a female very early on, and that was in Studio 54.

I was there with the girls and some other friends, and we were just freestyle dancing, having fun. I must have thrown out a body wave or something, not realizing it, because all of a sudden this tall female with curly black hair came walking across the dance floor, heading straight for me. She was backed up by a bunch of guys. She looked like she meant business, and I was actually excited at the prospect of battling a worthy female opponent. This was the first time I saw Peaches. I had no idea who she was at that time.

She was more of a locker than a popper, and she did this very strange move with her hand on her hip and a spin that reminded me of "I'm a little teapot." It must be her signature move, because she still does it today. Anyway, she had either greatly underestimated me or greatly overestimated herself, because with just a few moves she knew she had been beaten. She turned around and went back the way she came. She never tried to battle me again.

So speaking of Studio 54, The Dolls were there one night, and someone came over to us and said that Roseland, a very famous club which was once known for its ballroom dancing, was having a break dancing contest that night, and the prize was five thousand dollars. Now because we basically got into most night clubs for free and we did not drink alcohol, we did not carry too much cash. We did not have any contacts at Roseland, so we could not get in free, and the entry fee was more than we had on us. As we were trying to figure out what to do and fast, because we were running out of time, JaeCie came over to us and got us in a huddle.

She had just run into this guy she knew from around her way, and he asked her if she would hold onto his money. He had just got paid from his job, and he did not want to blow all his money on booze, women and other expensive items. He said he would get it back from her at the end of the night. Without saying a word, we looked at one another and ran for the door.

We got to Roseland and the break dance contest was in full swing. There had been a few crews who had already performed. How were they? I asked this guy. "Yo, they were whack," he told me. We went and put our names on the list to compete in the contest. The MC came over to us and asked us what song we wanted to dance to; we had forgotten to write one down. I looked at his clipboard with the sign-up sheet and I saw a whole bunch of names crossed off the list. Now I had asked one guy how many crews had performed already, and he told me a few, but yet I saw a whole bunch of crew's names crossed off. I asked the MC, why are those names crossed off the list? Did they go on already? He said, "No, they went off." He told us that as soon as the other female dance crews found out we were in the contest, they had dropped out, along with a couple of the B-Boy crews.

I wished they had not done that. We wanted more females to get out there, and just because you think someone else is better than you, you should still go out there and do your best—because you will not only feel good about yourself, but hey, you never know what is going to happen. Maybe we would have messed up badly. Maybe the crowd or the judges would have thought they had something we didn't. Maybe there was a talent scout or someone who liked them and had some other opportunities for them. Hey, it happened like that for us at the second big break dance contest at The Roxy.

The point is, no matter what, get out there and go for yours. You never know what you can accomplish if you do not try.

The Dynamic Dolls won the contest hands-down, and we rushed back to Studio 54 just in time to meet JaeCie's friend. He had been looking for us because he was leaving, and he wanted his money! Whew. I thought about how awkward it would have been if we had not won. We would have paid him back, just not that evening. It was still a nervy thing to do, though.

Another night I was hanging out with JaeCie in the Bronx where she lives. We were looking for something to do, but we had no money. I don't know why we did not have any money. We made good money and usually always had a check coming in from something we had done. All of our paychecks went to Headquarters, our manager's printing press business and "Dynamic Central," where Break Dance International operated. We would pick our money up there.

JaeCie found out that a club called "Ones" at 111 First Avenue was having a dance contest that night, and ladies got in free, so off we went. Surprise, guess who won! And it was a good thing too, 'cause we didn't even have money to get on the subway to get home. Now we had some cash, and we went out for breakfast.

I did not save a dime, but it's not like I made a million dollars anyway. I did give my mom a nice chunk of what I made, and a lot was spent on new outfits for us to perform in, or to wear to functions we were invited to. Like one night we had to make an appearance at this party in Manhattan. I don't even know who it was for or who the host was—all I know is it was a party, and there were models and photographers everywhere.

I was busy giving break dance lessons to a famous old-school singing group who had won the lessons at an auction that was held by Joe Holloway from the New Directions Theatre, Inc.

Till this day it drives me crazy, because I cannot remember the name of that group I gave break dance lessons to. All I know is they were big, I knew who they were because I liked their songs, and they sang R&B and later some disco. I still have a letter from the auction house. Maybe if they still exist, I can find the records of who won that particular auction.

So Susie Q went out to find us matching outfits for the evening's event. She had bought us these white jumpsuits with buckles here and there. The first thing I thought of was karate. But with the collar up and some high heels, it was all right—until she told me she paid a hundred-plus dollars for them, each! I was not happy, but we did look good, even in a room filled with models. Note: you can't really see them, but we are wearing them in the Dynamic group photo.

There was this other girl who was kind of a popper and she always acted as if she was my friend, but I knew she really did not like me. One weekend at the Fresh Club in Manhattan by Fourteenth Street and Union Square, I made mention that I was tired of popping and was thinking of giving it up (not). Well, she was so excited, but she tried to act concerned. Two weeks later I happened to go to the Fresh Club again, and I went upstairs and immediately saw a circle going. I went over to check it out, and who do you think was in the circle? Yes, the girl popper—and guess whose moves she was trying to do? Correct, mine!

So I was standing almost in her circle but behind her, so she couldn't see me yet. Her home girls were trying to get her attention to tip her off that I was standing behind her, but this girl was too busy trying her best to do my moves and she didn't notice. So as she was all happy about her circle and her new stolen moves, I stepped in behind her and started doing the same thing, only much better. When the crowd started going wild and laughing, she finally turned around. I wish I had a photo, because a picture is worth a thousand words. She was both shocked and embarrassed, not to mention busted and burned! Yes, Hazel, that was you.

Listen, any dancer who says they have never bit a move off another dancer is a liar. I myself took one of my signature moves off Spinner, my former crew member and boyfriend, I told you about him, from The Dynamic Rockers.

Heck, one of the biggest biters there ever was, happened to be Michael Jackson himself. He even bit a signature move of The Dolls that I made up. He does it in his video for "The Way You Make Me Feel," and you can see us do it in our video "The Beat Street Strut," filmed years before "The Way You Make Me Feel."

Now all you Michael Jackson fans, don't get mad at me for telling it like it is. It is well known that Michael Jackson used to watch all the singers when he was a kid and imitate their moves. Well, it is something he did throughout his entire career. All the old school Hip Hop people know that Michael Jackson did *not* invent the moonwalk, nor was he the first person to do it on television.

Little kids were doing the moonwalk all over, and there is a ton of video footage of B-Boys doing the moonwalk way before Michael ever did it. Actually, you can see many versions of the moonwalk in old black-and-white movies from the 1930s. From Fred Astaire to Dick Van Dyke, you can just see it being created right before your eyes.

What most people do not realize is many break dancing moves had already been executed decades before we were ever born. All you have to do is watch clips from the old black-and-white movies, and you will see many dancers both black and white doing mini swipes, footwork, and all kinds of break dancing moves. I couldn't believe my eyes when I was watching a movie from the 1930s, and at the very end of the movie a white kid runs down the sidewalk and does a few back handsprings. He then lands on his head and does a corkscrew head spin, right there on the sidewalk! I was stunned.

That movie is called "The Wild Boys of the Road." Frankie Durro is the name of the kid, and he was in a lot of movies back then. So you see, people have been biting other people's dance moves forever! Even today when I watch videos of battles or performances, I still see so many of Dynamic's moves being done. Many of our steps and moves are now staples for any B-Boy or B-Girl.

Even in popping I see some of my moves, some of Spinner's moves, Shake's moves, and so on. Because many of us created our own moves from the beginning when there were very few moves out there, it is safe to say that we helped shape popping, break dancing and footwork into what it is today. If you watch videos of many break dancing crews from 1983, you will see that these other crews did not have any choreographed routines, because Dynamic were the only ones who were doing it. And then if you watch videos from late 1984 and 1985, you will begin to see all of these other crews starting to do routines. The only problem was, they were using Dynamic's routines. People will say this is bull, but all you have to do is watch the videos. End of story!

Some of my earliest battles were when I was still hanging out at The Fun House and I had been popping for a little while. I was born and raised in Brooklyn, New York, and when word got around throughout the neighborhood about my skills, the neighborhood kids thought it was their job to bring every popper from the five boroughs and beyond to my house. After a while it became way too much, with them ringing the bell several times a day.

They would show up with these guys who wanted to battle me, and most of them were so whack. I remember this one day I had been out all night and the bell rang. My cousin told me they got some guy who came all the way from New Jersey to visit family and wanted to battle me. I could tell they were not going to leave me alone unless I came downstairs. I went down in my PJs, took one look at the kid, busted out some of my top moves, and then turned around and went back to bed.

After a while I had to put an end to this whole imposition. They weren't even bringing me worthy opponents. Almost all my battles were with guys. It would have been cool to have a great female opponent, one who really made me work for it, but there really weren't any back then. I'm glad that has all changed today.

The best battle I ever had took place in Coney Island, Brooklyn, I had gone to C.I. (as we call it) in the beginning of the summer, and one of the first things you see when you arrive in C.I. is the famous Cyclone rollercoaster. Right next to tho Cyclone is the Himalaya—it is one of those rides that goes real fast in a circle with a few hills, so you go up and down as you go round. The Himalaya had its own D.J. and he always played the dopest music, so there was usually a crowd of dancers by the Himalaya. That day was no exception.

I worked my way through the crowd so I could get a better look in the circle. There were a bunch of guys who looked like they were a popping crew who dominated the circle. Other people were jumping in the circle as well, so when the mood stuck, I got in on the fun too. Well I started popping, and all of a sudden these three dudes were all over me. They were throwing waves in my face and ticks; it was clear I was not well received. At this point in time I was an okay popper, and for a female a very good popper, but it was still new to me. We left the circle.

By the end of the summer, I was fresh! I had mad skills now, and I and my friend were going to Coney Island. When we arrived there was a pretty large crowd by the Himalaya, so we headed over. As luck would have it, those three guys I had faced the last time were there, and they were mostly dominating the circle. I told my friend to go ask the D.J. to put on "Buffalo Gals," which was my jam at the time. I headed off to have a little fun.

I hung back in the crowd for a bit and just watched the action when one of the dudes spotted me. They whispered to one another and they all started laughing, and it was on.

One by one they came into the circle and started getting in my face, like they did the last time, so I stepped in the circle. Now keep in mind that most of the people there were either black or Hispanic, so to see a white girl in the circle to begin with started the booing and hissing.

I went in and I started popping the same way I did when I first met these guys, and they were loving it! They were laughing and pointing and making fun of me. So I stepped out and one guy stepped in, I figured he was the leader and the best out of the three. He was again very aggressive and in my face. My turn. I stepped in the circle, and immediately the booing and hissing began. I did the same exact little popping routine I'd done just a minute ago, and now the entire crowd was laughing, saying, "Go home, white girl." I stepped out.

The same guy got back in and the crowd was cheering, I noticed he was repeating all of his moves, which usually meant he'd got no more moves. At this time I was looking at my friend up by the D.J.'s booth, and she was on her way back toward me. She shrugged her shoulders as if to say "*I don't know if he'll play it.*" There was no way I could go back in that circle again and do that routine again without getting a beat-down, so with or without my song, I had to go for it.

It was just like a movie, timed so perfectly. As he stepped out of the circle and I stepped in, I heard the "Eeeee, aye yi yi" beginning of Buffalo Gals. BAM! I went off!

Ticks, waves, gliding all over the place. Till this day I can still see that dude's mouth fall open. The crowd now exploded in applause and began hollering. People were buggin' the hell out. I dropped it all right there in their circle, and when I was done they were all over me, patting me on my back, shaking my hand. It was a great moment.

"Yo, you got me, you got me good." The guy was shaking his head, laughing. I pulled that little trick once or twice after that elsewhere, but it was never as great as it was that day. I still have a smile on my face as I am telling you this story. I like having fun, and it was a good time had by all.

That is my favorite battle story.

The Swatch Watch Fresh Fest Tour–1984

The Swatch Watch Fresh Fest Tour was the first Hip Hop tour of its kind. Never before had there been a multitude of talent, all under one roof at one time, as there were on this tour. The first of several tours to come had such artists as Run DMC, The Fat Boys, Kurtis Blow, Whodini, Newcleus—and of course, The Dynamic Breakers!

There were other dancers, such as Magnificent Force, Uptown Express and Jermaine Dupree. Yes, Jermaine Dupree, who was just a little kid back in 1984 and oh, so cute. Another tidbit of information which many people do not know is UTFO (Roxanne, Roxanne) was also on that tour, but you will not find their name on any of the advertisements. Why, you may ask? Because they were on that tour as backup dancers for Whodini. But it wouldn't be long until Doc Ice, Kangol Kid and The Educated Rapper would take center stage with their soon-to-be hit record, "Roxanne, Roxanne".

I was among the privileged few who got to hear that song while still in its prerecorded stages. Doc Ice had taken out a cassette tape and dropped it in a boom box, and told me he wanted to know what I thought of their rap they had done in a basement studio. Before it had even finished, I turned to Doc and said, "You got a hit on your hands." Now I am not saying I am some kind of musical psychic, but let me ask you—didn't you know the first time you heard "Roxanne" played on the radio that it was a hit?

Enough said.

There is a question I get asked a lot, and it has to do with The Dynamic Breakers headlining in The Fresh Fest Tour. Let me take you back a little bit.

The news was all over the place—the second Big Break Dance contest at The Roxy in NYC was coming. Now, the first Big Break Dance contest offered the first prize winners a part in the upcoming movie "Beat Street," which we all know The Dynamic Breakers won. This time the prize would be a spot on the upcoming Swatch Watch Fresh Fest Tour.

This time the competition was even fiercer than the first contest, because The Dynamic Breakers had raised the bar and the expectations for break dance crews were way up there. If you did not have a choreographed routine, you could forget about it, unless you had some amazing skills. Of course, The Dynamic Dolls were entering this contest.

Even with the cards stacked against us, The Dynamic Dolls had the highest scores out of the entire competition. How they worked it was each contestant would get scored by the judges. Two of the judges just happened to be Lady Blue, Rock Steady's manager, and Rose, manager of The Furious Rockers. So it was amazing that The Dolls had the highest score.

On the day of the last competition that would lead to the finals, we were about to step in front of the judges again. I noticed one of the Dolls, Susie Q, was very upset and angry. With no time to talk, I quickly asked her what was wrong and she told me she just had a big argument with Lady Blue. I had no idea at this point what had happened, but I was a little concerned that it may affect our chances, being that she was a judge. I was confident, however, that Susie Q would be a professional and do what we came there to do.

We began our new routine—we had to make sure we gave them something new and exciting to judge. Just a short time into our performance I heard words going back and forth between Lady Blue at the judges' table and Susie Q, who was dancing next to me.

What happened next changed the course of our careers, and not for the better. Susie Q walked out! She just up and walked away from our performance, away from our chances to not only be in the finals, but to probably win first place. We were disqualified! I cannot tell you how upset I was. I do not understand how those two managers were accepted as judges, especially when The Furious Rockers, one of their crews, was in the contest.

Well, I was not having it. I knew we would have won that contest, and so did everyone else. I had a plan. But first, since The Dynamic Dolls were disqualified from the contest, I decided to offer my choreography skills to The Furious Rockers. Why would I do such a thing, especially when their manager was one of the judges and my enemy? Because my man was in that crew and they were my friends, and if The Dolls could not win, I wanted them to win. I choroographed a routine with them using each crew member's specialty. The night had finally arrived.

I had told the Dolls to show up at The Roxy in our black and fluorescent colored outfits, and be ready to perform. "How are we going to do that?" they asked. "Don't worry about it, I got it all worked out," I told them. They may have been able to kick us out of the contest, but they could never kick us out of The Roxy. The Roxy was our home away from home. The owners of The Roxy had asked if we would consider them becoming our managers. We also brought a lot of business their way. So you see, there was no way we were going to be thrown out of The Roxy.

I had already spoken to the house D.J., Richie, and I explained the current situation to him. I told him he would be taking a chance that he may get in some trouble if he did this for us, and he was down regardless. My plan was to crash the contest and perform in front of the television cameras and the entire crowd. Even if we had no music, we were going to show everyone who would have won that contest—no disrespect to Furious.

Charles Stettler, who was The Fat Boys' manager and my friend, found out about my plan, but he begged me not to go through with it. He was concerned that we could get in trouble, even arrested. I thanked him for his concern for us, but I assured him nothing was going to stop us from performing that evening. This was about standing up for what was right and not accepting the raw deal we had been handed.

Charles asked me to just wait until he came back, just a few minutes. I had asked him why? He said, what is a few minutes going to change? If I'm not back, then you go ahead and do what you have to do. I agreed. As promised, Charles was back within a few minutes, and he said, "It was all fixed." I don't know who he had spoken to, but he said that we could go ahead with our performance as planned, as long as we knew that we would not be in the contest. We knew that was not going to happen, but we wanted the people to see us perform anyway, and let them wonder why *we* were not in the contest.

We took our place on the side of the stage. It was a raised platform and still looked like it did in the movie "Beat Street." Anyone who used to go to The Roxy before "Beat Street" was filmed knows that they built a whole new stage for the movie. We were waiting for The Tap Dance Kid to finish his performance. It was Alfonso Ribeiro.

When they announced us, many of the people in the crowd were a little confused. I know this because afterward they all wondered why we performed instead of competing in the contest, most of them stating, "You girls would have killed it and won." Tell us something we don't know.

Immediately after our performance, we were approached by several people who had one offer or another. On the spot we were photographed for a magazine, I think it was Glamour—who remembers, we were in so many of the major magazines back then, including Ebony, a Teen magazine, and we even had a spread in the centerfold of The Muppet Magazine, just to name a few.

We also did a commercial for anti-smoking, and other offers were handled by our managers. So my decision to crash the contest was a successful one, even though they did not show us in the final broadcast.

The photograph on the following page was taken the night of the contest and appeared in Glamour magazine.

TRY IT

Lace your "kicks" (sneakers) the breakdance way: Criss-cross laces underneath the tongue, threading laces straight across on top. Bring lace ends up through last eyelets and tie.

There were several different winners of the Swatch Watch Break Dance contest in different categories. The Furious Rockers won first prize for best break dance crew, Uptown Express won for electric boogie crew (although they had been using the same routine they did on Star Search years earlier), and Magnificent Force were also winners.

Here is the question I get asked all the time:

"How is it that The Dynamic Breakers were the lead break dance crew on the Swatch Watch Fresh Fest tour, when The Furious Rockers won the contest and they were not ever on that tour?"

It was management's fault.

Mr. Speed, the president of The Furious Rockers, told me that it was their manager, Rose, who ruined their chances of being on the Swatch Watch tour because of greed. Knowing her, that is not difficult to believe. I bet she tried to incorporate herself as a performer as well.

(Left) D-Roc – Rubberband – Rock – Eddie – Ringo - Mr. Speed NYC '84 Winners of the Roxy Breaking Contest

114

The Dynamic Dolls were not on the Swatch Watch Fresh Fest tour either. The only reason I was there was because one of the guys, Flip, had broken his foot and he could not perform. The natural choice to take his place was me, Kim-A-Kazi. Not only could I do Flip's job of spinning the guys on my head and doing the 3-man spin, but I knew all of the routines, and I added one thing that The Dynamic Breakers did not have—an expert popper. I was able to get The Dynamic Dolls to perform for a few of the shows on the tour, but there was no pay. It was mostly for exposure. It was at my insistence that The Dolls were able to perform. However, it meant double duty for me.

I would perform with the guys first, then I would run back to the dressing room and change, cool down a bit, and then go back on stage and do a whole other performance with The Dynamic Dolls. It was exhausting, but it was worth it. We had a big scare during one of those performances with The Dolls. JaeCie was out front doing her solo and she went into her head spins, and she had spun too close to the edge of the stage and went right over the edge! This stage was a good eight feet or more off the ground. I remember being so afraid that I was going to find her with her neck broken or her head split open. When I got to the end of the stage, she was already getting back up and making her way back onto the stage. Whew—I forgot she was Dynamic!

I myself almost went over the edge of that stage. Not while on my head, but on my knees. It was funny, during the routine with the guys we were doing floor work, and then we would all do kick-ups (where you kick up from lying on your back, and then you are standing). Well, during my kick-up I used too much power, and I did land on my feet, but the momentum sent me forward and down on my knees, and I slid on my knees across the stage straight toward the edge. I can still recall worrying I was going to go right off the stage, but I came to a stop right at the very edge—and then I threw my arms open and went "ta-dah" like I meant to do that. The audience went wild!

Listen, you always have to be prepared to mess up. The difference between screwing up and making it work for you is a good sense of humor, and trying to plan ahead of time when you practice to come up with another move if your first one doesn't go right. It takes away something when a dancer messes up, and then highlights the fact that they messed up by not recovering quickly. A great dancer is prepared for mistakes and is able to recover immediately by going directly into another move without hesitation. To me, it is the difference between a good dancer and a great dancer. To a dancer, it may be the difference between winning and losing.

For example, when the guys were rehearsing for a show they were doing with Penny Marshall called "The New Show" (it is on YouTube) Ms. Marshall was having trouble with some of the moves. The Dolls had gone to the studio to meet up with the guys, so we were watching them practice. I noticed Ms. Marshall struggling to do some of the moves, and as usual, I could not keep my mouth shut. I had told the guys a suggestion, and this woman who was standing off to the side said to me, "You come here and show me what you mean." I was hesitant because I did not want to step on the guys' toes, but they gave me the go-ahead. Being a female, there are little tricks I learned that helped a B-Girl do some of the B-Boy moves, especially if she does not have the muscle power to do those moves. I showed Ms. Marshall these little tricks, and she started to improve.

I also noticed that when she tried to do a head spin, she took a long time to get her balance once up in a headstand, so I suggested that she part her legs and one of the guys would flip through her legs, giving her a few extra seconds to gain her balance. We also came up with some other moves she could go into, just in case she could not pull off the head spin. Ms. Marshall showed us a few of her own little moves, which she wound up doing after her head spin failed. (See @ 2:20 on the video on YouTube)

Remember, no matter if you are in a battle or a performance, you cannot look incompetent. Always be prepared with an alternate move, just in case the move you are doing does not come off. This way it looks like you meant to do that move and did not fail.

That woman who asked me to show Penny Marshall how to fix her moves was world-renowned choreographer Patricia Birch. If you are not familiar with either of these people, Penny Marshall is an award-winning director/producer, and she was best known as Laverne DeFazio from the award-winning television show "Laverne & Shirley," which was a spinoff from their appearances on "Happy Days." Patricia Birch was the woman who choreographed the movies "Grease" and "Grease 2." Patricia's resume is extensive and impressive, and it was Patricia who was hired to work on the music video "The Beat Street Strut."

Kim-A-Kazi spinning Kano on her head @ The Fresh Fest 1984

JaeCie & Kim on our tour bus and posing with Mighty Whitey Fresh Fest

We were all to meet in Manhattan to get on the bus. It was like a Greyhound bus with a restroom aboard. It wasn't until we reached the first arena on the tour that we all got our own tour buses.

Waiting to board our tour bus

(L) Flip, Duce and Kim·A·Kazi

Outside our hotel–Dynamic practicing by our tour bus. We were always improving our moves and our routines while having fun.

Mag Force: Joe Flash – Shalamar – Steve are practicing too

Charles Stettler (manager of The Fat Boys) also hanging out with us

Joe Simmons, A.K.A Run, A.K.A. Rev Run from Run DMC, watching Dynamic practicing in the parking lot.

Kim-A-Kazi and The Dynamic Breakers @ Fresh Fest tour

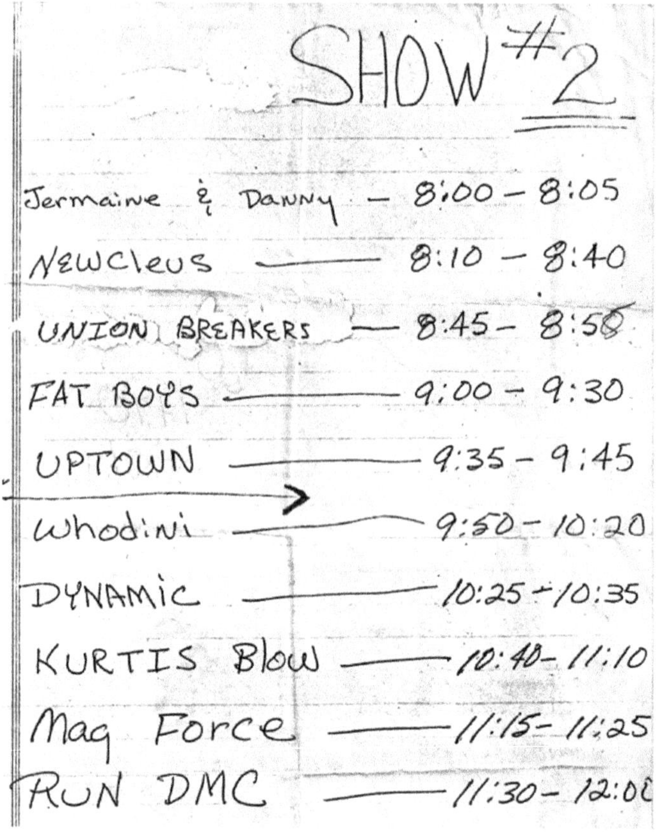

SHOW #2

Jermaine & Danny — 8:00 – 8:05

Newcleus — 8:10 – 8:40

UNION BREAKERS — 8:45 – 8:50

FAT BOYS — 9:00 – 9:30

UPTOWN — 9:35 – 9:45

Whodini — 9:50 – 10:20

DYNAMIC — 10:25 – 10:35

KURTIS Blow — 10:40 – 11:10

Mag Force — 11:15 – 11:25

RUN DMC — 11:30 – 12:00

This is the performance schedule from the 2ⁿᵈ show on the Swatch Watch Fresh Fest 1984 tour. Each act performed as scheduled above. Subject to change.

122

1. Honey Begining - Kane & A. Born (Chill out)
2. Spider Kim & Deuce (Wild Style)
3. Kane & Airborn
4. Kim Solo
5. Turn Around Dives
6. Spider
7. Kim + Airborn - Prepola
8. Kano
9. Spide & A.Born (R & J.)
10. Deuce
11. Airborn
12. 3 man
13. End Routine

A quick memo passed around to each member of Dynamic so we knew what routine we would be performing that evening. We would name our routines, so at any time all we had to do was call out a name and every member of our crew, including The Dolls, would go into that routine at a moment's notice.

Note: On the following page you will see another example of our putting together a routine plan. What was great about this was even if someone had already seen our performance, we would try to switch things around for the next performance. I can take credit for making up a routine one time in the ladies' room during a special performance at The Waldorf Astoria's Starlight room. I created a new routine in the ladies' room within five minutes. Impressive? Perhaps, but I feel it was also impressive that my sister Doll, Susie Q, was picking up the routine in five minutes and performing it flawlessly.

Susie Q and I had an uncanny sense of timing. When we danced together, especially in the later years, we danced as one. The funny thing was, when we danced freestyle, our styles could not have been more different than one another's—but when we performed together, we were spot on. (See photo below)

A perfect example of Susie Q and myself always being in sync: Before the picture was snapped, I said to Susie Q, "Do the Roxy," and Bam! We are almost identical (referring to photo on page 124).

This was not planned or staged; it was spontaneous. The photo was taken in Italy.

I have a lot of respect for Susie Q as a dancer. She learned quickly, and she had such exuberance when she danced. When I was filled with excitement and adrenaline when I danced, it came across as unleashed power and my moves were too hard and pronounced, which I did not like. With Susie Q, she seemed to pick up speed when she was excited and was very bubbly. We each had our own style, but somehow it worked when we danced side by side.

Kim try to stick in words

walk to spot spin stop
slap hands, Do (I Don't know) it
up feet work down, spin
foot work into kick ups
Rockabar routine into relays
go back.
Susie & Brenda kertweel att
to feet work.
JaeCie, Denise + Kim boogie
routine in back ground
JaeCie + Kim flip ½ + Brenda
over shoulder.
Denise goes out then JaeCie
then me AND Susie - head
spin. Brenda sic
is enough time foot work everyone
then three men Double hand
Glides — the end

Last line says: "If enough time; footwork- everyone then the 3
man–double hand glides (Kim-A-Kazi & Susie Q) the end…" This
was an early routine, before we found JaeCie.

Chapter 11 – The Beat Street Strut Video

Our manager received a call, and Patricia Birch wanted us to be in a video that she was hired to work on: "The Beat Street Strut." In the beginning Patricia wanted me to play the part of the female who was trying to learn how to break dance. After thinking about it, I declined, because if I was to do that role then The Dynamic Dolls would not only be incomplete, but they would not be able to do our lifts without me. Because my crew was more important than having the spotlight on myself, I politely declined.

Patricia had no problem with my decision and asked me if I would help teach the girl who was going to do that role how to break dance. I agreed. Well, I did not know what I was getting myself into, for this girl really had no B-Girl skills at all. I tried to teach her easiest moves, like basic up-rock and footwork. I also tried to show her some popping moves, and then settled for a few simple Tut moves. I had to teach her how to do the Worm for the piece at the end where she dances with The Dynamic Breakers. I must admit, the role would have looked better if I'd done it myself, being a more experienced break dancer.

Patricia asked us for another favor—to be the judges for the auditions they were holding for additional dancers for the video. We were glad to do it. This actually gave us the opportunity to have some of our friends in the video, and to give some other kids who may not have ever gotten the chance to be in a music video the opportunity. I believe that we were very fair, however! I do wonder to myself what we would have decided, if what happened next had played all the way through.

Okay, The Dolls were seated behind the judges' table and we had been viewing dancers all day long, when all of a sudden, the door opens and in walks The Rock Steady Crew! They were all sheepskin down and had some females with them. No sooner did they walk into the room when they spotted us at the judges' table. There were still some of the crew who had not made their way into the room, yet the ones who walked in the door kind of stopped the moment they saw us. Without speaking a word, they simply turned around and walked out!

Now I cannot honestly say what we would have done if they'd stayed and performed. Given the chance to reflect at this moment, I guess I would have to say we would not have picked them, only because this was our video. On the other hand, I think it may have been cool to have Dynamic and the RSC in the same video. I can honestly say, at that time, we enjoyed that little moment immensely!

All right, don't get your panties all in a bunch. First of all, we were still teenagers, you know, and secondly we were rivals—kind of like the New York Yankees and the Boston Red Sox (Dynamic being the Yankees, of course).

Both The Dynamic Breakers and Dolls had tours set up before we could film The Beat Street Strut video. The Dolls had a five-week tour in the French Antilles; meanwhile, the guys were going on The Pepsi Tour with Michael Jackson! I think our manager booked the Caribbean tour for all of us, and then the Pepsi tour opportunity came up, so he sent The Dolls off to the Caribbean with a replacement crew, The Fresh Kids, and the Dynamic Breakers got to perform with the Jacksons.

We returned from a grueling tour in the Caribbean just in time to do the Beat Street Strut video. It was the day after we returned! We didn't even have time to get our outfits from Puma, another one of our sponsors, so they had them sent to us on location, where we changed into our specially made pink Puma suits! Pink was my color, so the suits were made in pink. I don't think the other Dolls cared.

We had to be on location early in the morning, and everyone was warned that if you were late, filming would begin as scheduled—and without you. That is why we were one Doll short in the first scene on the stoop. JaeCie joined us shortly after. As for the fourth Doll, that was one of the guy's girlfriends, Smiley. She wasn't a regular Doll, she was an honorary Doll for that day, and because she had watched us practice so many times, she knew the routine we were doing and joined us. She is the one wearing the orange.

It was a long day and I was suffering because of my right knee. I had developed a bad case of water on the knee while on the Caribbean tour, and I had to bow out of the last show there. However, because we were under contract with JVC Electronics and they were demanding a full performance, I had no choice but to perform all shows. I will tell you, that was the one thing that was both good and bad about being "the only one" able to do a special feat. No one could take my place. So all day my right knee was not only all swelled up, but it was killing me.

You may be able to notice the problem with my right knee when I am spinning Susie Q on my head in the video. The spot where we were dancing was slanted and sloped, which usually would be no problem for me. I could spin anyone on my head just about any place, but with my knee being in the condition it was, you can see my right leg is off as I am trying to compensate for the pain and the uneven surface we were dancing on. After filming ended for the day, I went over Shake's house and wound up sleeping over on the couch, as I had done many times before. The next morning, "Mom"—Shake's mother—had to call my family to come get me, because I was sick and felt faint and my right leg had locked up. I could no longer bend it.

My mother made me go to the hospital, which I would usually never do, and the doctor told my mother that this was the worst case of water on the knee he had ever seen. He had treated football players and carpenters, and none were as bad as mine. It just goes to show you that when I do something, I like to be the best at it!

Back to the video. As I said, it was a long day, but we did have our fun too. During a lunch break, a bunch of the dancers had made a circle and were dancing, of course. My girl Susie Q had joined in an up-rock battle with this dude Klown, I was passing by on my way to do something and Klown started to call me out. "Nah," I waved my hand as I kept walking. He kept prodding me on, so just to shut him up, I went over. We began to up·rock, and he was doing a few nasty gestures toward me. So on the third time, on the way down up·rocking, I took his pants with me, leaving Klown standing there in his drawers with his pants around his ankles. I walked away while the crowd exploded with laughter and applause. I must say, that was brilliant. You must remember—back then, most moves were new. Compared to today's moves, it wouldn't be so great.

When the video was finally released, I was livid! They had cut all of our best moves out. Hand glides, floats, popping, head spins—none of those moves were in there. Even with our guys, they showed one of Duce's failed corkscrew head spins, which was a rarity. Duce had some of the best head spins out there, along with Float and Kid Freeze and a few others. In addition, they cut out most of the guys' best moves as well. I joke around saying that the "old man" you see in the second half of the video was in it more than I was.

The one thing that was pretty cool about being the "stars" of the video was we did get special treatment. We had our own trailer on site, fully equipped with kitchen, bathroom and a bedroom. The Dolls had our own makeup staff and wardrobe people. It was funny, because they really did call "*makeup*" and they would come running, dusting our faces with makeup and fixing our hair, even though I didn't really need it with my short hair.

There is even a little story behind the humongous glasses I am wearing at the end of the video. My manager Cord bought me those glasses for my birthday to replace a pair that was stolen out of our locked dressing room in the Caribbean. I had purchased my original glasses—pink, of course—during our first trip to Italy, when I had no idea how the currency exchange worked. Back in 1983, I paid eighty·five American dollars for those glasses. Who knew? I thought they were around fifteen. They were Carreras, and I have a photo of me wearing them. They looked nothing like their replacement pair, but I guess they were the only pair of pink Carrera glasses he could find. Cord asked me if I was going to wear them in the video, I had not planned on ever wearing them, but I did not want to hurt his feels or seem ungrateful, so I wore them.

Note: Many years ago, I took a chance and contacted Patricia Birch. She was so sweet to not only remember who I was, but she actually sent me a copy of The Beat Street Strut video from her own copy. It was not a very good copy, but I was thrilled to have it. This was way before the Internet or YouTube existed. I have been trying ever since to obtain copies of many of the other performances we did, but with no luck so far.

It is beyond my comprehension as a human being that anyone could purposely withhold footage or any memories of someone's career, especially someone who is supposed to be your friend. These are the kind of mean actions that give people bad karma. It is a cruel thing to do.

And it didn't just happen to me, unfortunately. It happens more than people realize.

Scenes from "The Beat Street Strut" Video. (Top: Kim-A-Kazi, Susie Q)

Kim-A-Kazi spinning Dolls JaeCie & Susie Q

Freeze frame from video - R to L: Kim-A-Kazi – JaeCie - Susie Q - Smiley

Freeze frame—notice the huge Carrera glasses on me?

Top: This is me wearing the Carrera glasses I purchased in Italy, that were stolen just minutes after this picture was taken.

Bottom: Kim-A-Kazi and Susie Q backstage before a performance in Italy.

Chapter 12—Going on Tour

Going on tour can be a lot of fun, but it is a lot of hard work too. We had very little down time to enjoy ourselves and sight-see. When you are inner-city kids, you rarely get to go anywhere outside of your own neighborhood, and yet here we were traveling all over the world and we rarely were able to enjoy it. However, it was a great experience to see how other people lived, and to walk on white sandy beaches with water so clear you could see straight down to the bottom.

For me, one of the hardest things to deal with at times was the different foods. I am what you would call a picky eater, and although I have branched out as I have aged, I was terribly picky back then. I must have lost a lot of weight while in the Caribbean, especially in Guyana. Everything was curry this and curry that. I swore I would never eat anything curried again in my life, and I have kept that promise. Too bad I was too young to appreciate seafood back then, with every kind of seafood you could imagine as fresh as it could be. My idea of seafood back then was some fish sticks from Mrs. Paul or Gorton's from our freezer.

Even during our tours in Italy, I did not appreciate the authentic Italian cooking. My mom makes a great sauce by anyone's standards, and there are still some authentic Italian foods I do not appreciate. However, now that I am older, there are many dishes I would appreciate having. I do hope to visit Italy again one day with my husband and take in all of the culture, food and history. There is just one thing I did not enjoy then and would not appreciate today, and that is *vino*—wine. I don't really drink alcohol, but I will never drink wine, I just do not like it.

The one great thing about having sponsors is they pay for everything! When we were in Martinique, we had run up a bar tab you would not believe, and none of us drank alcohol! I remember Susie Q discovering this new drink there called "Orangina." Some of you may remember that drink, but it had not made it to the United States at that time. We found out too late that the hotel stopped serving food early, so I think you had a few hours after dinner was served to order room service. We returned one night after a show and we were starving, but there was no place to get food at our hotel at that hour. I believe it was around 10 p.m. 1 was getting ready to go to sleep when the guys came to our door—The Fresh Kids, who were on this tour with us. They said they were off to find some place to get something to eat. After all, we'd just finished a performance and our young, active bodies needed nourishment. What happened next was an adventure.

I was wearing a long nightshirt that came down past my knees, and I had a pair of socks on my feet. "We are just going across the road," they said. "You do not need to get dressed or wear shoes." So I left as-is. We walked across the road toward a small restaurant someone had told the guys about. But when we got there, the place was closed. A man walking by told us we could find a truck that sold food just down the road a bit. He said it was parked outside a night club. Just down the road, ha!

We walked and we walked down this road of dirt and rocks, and there was nothing but darkness and the woods on both sides of us. We were now on a mission and had gone too far to turn back in defeat. As we marched along, we were suddenly surrounded by a pack of wild dogs! Barking, growling and snarling at us, we were gathered in the center of these mad dogs, who were just as hungry as we were. Hey, we are from New York—we'd been in more dangerous situations than this. We all grabbed large sticks and branches, and some grabbed rocks, and we fought off the pack of wild dogs. Some of them retreated back into the woods, and some just stood back and begrudgingly let us pass, while still barking in protest of the outcome.

The road ahead was long, dark, and there was not a sign of life. Just as we were about to give up, we noticed the road split, and off to the right were some lights. As we made our way around the bend, it was if we had crossed over from dark and death to life! There was loud music and the sound of people laughing, and the smell of cooking food was being carried in a thick cloud of smoke right toward us. We were like savages who had not eaten in days. They offered one thing, and one thing only—blood burgers.

Back at the hotel there was a little hut by the pool where they barbequed food. The hamburgers were made out of who knows what, and they were served one way, Rare—so we named them blood burgers. We were never so happy to eat one of those blood burgers as we were that night.

With our bellies full, we started our trek back to the hotel. It had just hit us of how far we had walked, and none of us were happy to repeat the trip. If there was any indication of how far we walked and how difficult the terrain was, all you had to do was look down at my feet. Yes, you could now see my feet, for the only evidence that remained that proved I was wearing socks when we began this trip were on my legs above the ankles. The socks had been torn and worn away from my feet.

As we walked back toward our hotel, we were approaching the area where we were attacked by the pack of wild dogs—and guess what? There they were, almost as if they were waiting for us. Just as we began gathering sticks to ward them off, a car approached. The guy stopped and after a brief explanation of what we were doing there, he was kind enough to give us a ride back to our hotel. Whew, what a relief that we didn't have to walk any further, and we did not have to fight off those wild dogs.

We arrived at our hotel just as the sun was rising and the hotel was setting up for breakfast. We all silently wondered if it was worth walking several miles to eat blood burgers, when we could have stayed in our warm beds for a few more hours to awake and have breakfast. Too late now.

The next day after lunch, Susie Q and I decided to make a plate of breads, fruit and cookies to take up to our room, so we would have something to eat when the place closed at night. As we walked out of the dining area with our plate of goodies, a hotel employee stopped us. Can you believe that they confiscated the food from us? Talk about embarrassing. Well, this food issue was not just a problem in Martinique. We found the same problem in Guyana.

In Guyana, we were basically in the jungle! The lobby and dining area had a ceiling, but not four walls. The majority of the ground floor was open and the jungle was just yards away. Bats flew through the entire first floor, and the guard told us that cattle and all kinds of animals wandered into the dining area and the lobby at night. So one night after a performance, we were all starving. This time my manager was in on it too.

We had to come up with a plan to get past the guard and into the kitchen to get something to eat. Susie Q and I were to distract the guard, while Cord and the guys snuck into the kitchen to get some food. So me and Susie Q went downstairs and started talking and flirting with the guard, and the guys snuck down the back stairway and began crawling on the floor, on their hands and knees. Now not only did we have to keep the guard distracted, but we had to get him to turn his back so he wouldn't see the guys and keep ourselves from laughing hysterically at the sight of the guys crawling across the floor. Once they were safe behind the bar and could crawl without being seen, we could relax a little.

We had to keep the guard's back turned so he would not see the doors to the kitchen opening, but he kept turning back around to survey the dining room, which was the area he was supposed to watch the most.

With a language barrier and only so much flirting that could be done without someone getting touchy-feely, the situation was becoming very uncomfortable. All of a sudden, the quiet night was filled with loud, blaring alarms, bells and whistles screaming like crazy. The guard gave us a look that said he knew we distracted him, and then he jumped into action and started running toward the kitchen doors. At the same time, Cord and the guys came running out of the kitchen doors and took off behind the bar as the guard was running toward the kitchen on the opposite side on the bar.

Meanwhile, Susie Q and I took off up the stairs and toward our room.

I don't think there was any real trouble, just a talking-to and a lecture for Cord from hotel management. But it was funny—ah, the things you will do when you are hungry. Trust me, I know I have done a few crazy things back in Brooklyn growing up when we were hungry.

Dynamic Dolls with the Fresh Kids (Poncho-Rudy-Chico)

Still in Guyana, we were asked if we would do an interview on their number one radio station, and they asked if any of us could rap. Well, I had written a rap for The Dolls a long time before, so that was no problem. So I went to the Fresh Kids and asked if any of them could rap, and if they had an original rap of their own. Chico said that he had a couple of his own raps he had written, so he was our man.

After all of the introductions, (Susie Q, Chico and I were brought into a large room that was empty except for the desks and three chairs that faced the control room. It was a little strange, because the show began and one of the announcers was speaking for a long time, and we had no idea what he was saying. The only thing I understood was our name, and they called break dancing "Le Smurf"—that always makes me laugh. Anyway, then the other announcer would translate their questions for us in English.

Everything was going well, and then the time came when they asked us if we would please demonstrate our rapping skills for them. They played a general beat for us to rap to. I started it off and Susie Q chimed in, because the rap I was doing was about The Dynamic Dolls, and we each had our own solo. We did our thing and we could tell they were pleased with our skills, for they were smiling and clapping along. Now it was Chino's turn to rap.

He sounded a little nervous, but for the first few lines his rap was okay. Then he started doing something that we had never heard before. He was "bleeping" himself! His rap had curse words in it, and instead of just changing the bad words, he kept saying, "Beep."

So let's just say the line was: "I'm as bad as they come but I got class, and all you sucker MC's can just kiss my 'beep'." Well, that was all Susie Q could take, and she began giggling her "beep" off. I looked at him in disbelief and tried to get him to look at me, so I could signal for him to stop beeping himself, but he would not look at me—and then, thank goodness, he was finished. I picked it up and began my rap, but Susie Q was still laughing and unable to control herself, so I did that one solo.

It was Chico's turn again and I figured here was his chance to redeem himself. Boy, was I wrong. He started doing the *same rap* he just did before, beeps and all. Well, by now Susie Q had slid under the table and was laughing her ass off.

There I was, smack in the middle of this beeping fool and Chuckles, and that was it for me. I could no longer contain myself and I joined Susie Q under the table, laughing like two hyenas'. Chico soon joined us. Well, the announcers were furious. I don't know what they were yelling, thank goodness, but they were yelling and flailing their arms about, and then basically threw our asses out of the studio.

At this point we really didn't care. We were exhausted and hot. Man, is it muggy over there, and break dancing in that heat and muggy weather is exhausting. We did however need to care about what our manager was going to say. He was waiting outside in the parking lot for us. We walked out of the radio station and a wall of heat slammed us. We looked like three little kids who did something wrong and were about to face their parents.

Cord was sitting in the car with the driver's side door wide open, and the radio was on. We could hear the announcer was still carrying on and I wanted to laugh so badly, but I did not dare. When we arrived at his car, all of us silent, Cord burst out laughing himself! He loved it and he did not care. He knew we were exhausted and we had been working so hard. You see, we did not just have to perform at all these different venues, but we had to practice as well. Then you have to do television interviews, newspaper and sometimes magazine interviews, and radio shows. Sometimes you have to do publicity meet-and-greets, and with one after another for all of those weeks—well, we were done. Not to mention I had that big water on my knee problem.

That was not the only performance we messed up on that trip. There was another.

We had been invited to a very fancy restaurant by the owner, and we were so glad that we could sit and relax and have a nice meal without having to worry about rushing off to do a show. We had finished our dinner and I spotted Cord speaking to the owner, and they shook hands. I knew something was up. Well as usual, Cord had volunteered us to do a free show for him. Adjoining the restaurant was a small room that consisted of a dance floor and seating on either side. The room itself was shaped like a football with seats that elevated like bleachers.

The Fresh Kids absolutely refused to do another freebie, and they were not obligated to do so. Being that Cord was not their manager and they had fulfilled all of their scheduled performances, there was really nothing Cord could do about it, so it was up to me and Susie Q. We were not happy about it either, and we did not blame The Fresh Kids for refusing, but to keep the peace, Susie Q and I headed to the dance floor.

Now keep in mind that we had just finished a big meal, and we were tired and had not planned on performing that evening. We began one of our routines, and when it came time for me to spin Susie on my head, we would separate to opposite sides of the dance floor, then do a little foot work routine, and then Susie Q would run to me where I would lift her up in the air. Before the bad injury to my left arm, I used to life the person up in the air and hold them above me with one arm while spinning, then I would lower them onto my head and spin them with no hands. But now I could not do that, so I just put them onto my head.

Just as we were doing the foot work, I saw Susie Q going slow, and then I realized she was laughing. Knowing her the way I do, I already knew what the situation was. I began chuckling, trying so hard to maintain control, for this time we had an audience and they were just a few feet away from us. Now came the time when Susie Q would run toward me so I could lift her into the air and onto my head. That did not happen.

Susie Q was now laughing so hard she couldn't walk, never mind run, so she staggered toward me. Now I was laughing, because although I knew what Susie Q was doing, I could see the crowd reacting to it. What was she doing? She was farting! The people closest to her had recoiled with that look on their faces. Some of them held their noses, while others waved their hands furiously under them, trying desperately to rid themselves of the terrible odor.

The rest of the crowd did know yet know what was going on but soon realized something was up, because Susie, who was supposed be jumping up so I could lift her, was now standing in front of my face laughing hysterically, and so was I. I lifted her up awkwardly and placed her on my head, but instead of Susie's body being perfectly straight so we looked like the letter "T", Susie Q was just hanging there on top of my head, and we looked more like an arrow. I started spinning, hoping that the momentum would cause Susie's body to straighten out and salvage this disaster of a performance, but no such luck.

This time Cord was furious and went off on us, but you know what? We did not give a crap. He had made too many promises and favors without consulting us first. After all, we were the ones who had to bust our butts, not him. He realized he was wrong—especially after we told him he was wrong—and he did not volunteer our services any more. On that trip, at least, there would be a few more "favors."

During this Caribbean tour, which was just around five weeks, I would say we had just a few days off. Sometimes it was only a half-day off. On this one day we had off, we were in Martinique. The man from JVC had a daughter who was about ten years old, and she was our little guide for the day. However, all we really wanted to do was relax on the beach. The hotel that we were staying at was a Club Med resort, so there we a lot of people there. We were able to access all of the amenities and we ate at the huge buffets they provided. We also got to use the non-motorized water crafts.

Our young guide took us down to the beautiful white sand beach, just steps away from our rooms. We were applying our lotion when I noticed many people were looking at us. People walking by, people on nearby blankets, and that usually meant that they recognized us—but this seemed different, for there were just too many diversified people looking at us. I asked the young girl why everyone was staring at us. Her English wasn't all that great and she struggled to translate. Finally, showing signs of frustration, she ripped off her bathing suit top. Both Susie Q and I looked at one another, our mouths hanging open in shock.

The little girl pointed to our bikini tops, and then to the people. In other words, she was telling us that the people were looking at us because we were wearing our bikini tops, and they knew we were visitors. We looked around, and she was right—not one other females was wearing a bathing suit top. I didn't care who was looking at us. I was not taking off my bathing suit top—yet. As the sun climbed higher in the sky, it became very hot, so we decided to get one of those foot pedal boats and go out on the water.

The water was so beautiful, you could see clear to the bottom of the ocean floor. When we were pretty far out,

Susie and I looked around and saw there wasn't anyone near us, so we finally took off our tops. We sat back taking the sun as our craft floated on the calm water. I decided to take a dip in the beautiful blue water, so in I dove. I was really enjoying myself swimming around, and I rested by hanging onto the large float that held up our craft. I was talking to Susie when I looked down into the water and saw a school of beautiful fish, all colors. All of a sudden I heard that terrifying sound—*dah dum, dah dum, dah dum dah dum dah dum dah dum dah dum.*

The music from the movie *Jaws.* I know a lot about sharks and was well aware that they were in these waters. I got so scared that a shark was going to grab me at any moment that I tried to pull myself out of the water, but the float was wet and slippery and I slipped back into the water. I was wet too, so when I pulled myself up a second time, I slipped and the jagged seam on the float scraped my stomach so badly that I was left with a deep purple scrape that was an inch wide and went from just under my breasts down to my lower stomach. I had never seen anything like it before. There was blood just under the skin, and the blood was purple, almost like when you get a bad bruise. Anyway, it hurt.

Another time we got brave and took off our tops on the beach, and I tell you, no one was paying us any mind. When we went to take a dip in the water, The Fresh Kids came on the beach and were yelling and laughing as they twirled our bikini tops in the air. Susie and I ducked under the water and demanded they put our tops down and move on. They gave us a hard time for a few minutes, and then they moved on. We never took our tops off again. That was about it for our time off in Martinique.

No matter where we went, it was always exciting to see new places and people, even when we toured from state to state. We have been to so many places, I could never mention them all. Each place has its own story, its own adventures, and I will always be grateful that I had the opportunity to travel to all of them.

Chapter 13—Commercials

We already know that I lost out on the Mountain Dew commercial due to sabotage, and the jury is still out on the Pony commercial, but as far as I know, I just wasn't what they were looking for when it came to the Hershey commercial. I actually lost out on a commercial because my feet were too big!

True dat, people. It was after I had stopped break dancing, and I received a call from my former manager telling me I was asked to moonwalk for a commercial. I don't even remember what the commercial was for, so I headed off to Manhattan, stood on a countertop and did the moonwalk about a hundred times. They loved my moonwalk. However, my size eight sneakers were too big for their commercial. Oh, well.

The two commercials we did were both filmed to be shown overseas, I have the feeling I am forgetting another commercial that we did, but for now I just remember these two.

Panasonic

Me, Susie and Duce were chosen to do a commercial for Panasonic with the great Peter Allen. I was the only one of us who knew right off the bat who he was. A flamboyant performer who was a singer, songwriter, composer and piano player, he is best known for his song; "When my baby, when my baby smiles at me, I go to Rio De Janeiro." And he was married to Liza Minelli, whom I also worked with.

We began in downtown Brooklyn, somewhere around Orange and Pineapple Streets. We got to meet Peter Allen in our trailer, where he asked us more questions than we asked him. He was a very nice person and he loved to laugh, which is great except for when you are outside freezing without a coat and Mr. Allen kept ruining the takes by laughing. We had a great time, but Susie and I must have done our little dance routine a hundred times, and it comes to the point where you have to try and keep up your energy and perform just as good as you did the take before, because you never know if this take is going to be a print.

I never did get to see the finished commercial, for after we wrapped up our part, they were filming the rest of the commercial under the Brooklyn Bridge, where they had Peter Allen's red piano waiting for him. I can barely remember hearing something about them wanting Duce to do backspins or head spins on the piano while Peter played. As I said, I never saw the commercial. A friend recently found a two-second clip of us onsite where we filmed that commercial, but I have yet to find the entire commercial. I am still hopeful it will turn up someday.

The second commercial we did was filmed in Times Square, New York City, also in 1984. All I know was it was a commercial against cigarette smoking, and it too would be aired overseas in another country. We never did get to see that commercial either.

I'll never forget—I was running late because of the traffic in Manhattan, and I had taken a cab to get there quicker. I could see the crew and the cameras set up from my cab and I was going to just get out there and walk the rest of the way, but the cab driver assured me we would be there in a minute, as soon as he made the next left turn. Well he couldn't make a left turn for several blocks, so I finally got out and ran.

When I arrived on site we began immediately, and the ironic part was the whole time we were filming, I was dying for a cigarette! Because I was in the taxicab and had to run a few blocks, I had no time to smoke a cigarette, plus I was nervous and upset because I was going to be late. Anyone who smokes knows what I am talking about. I was the only real smoker in our crew. A few of the guys indulged occasionally, and one of the guys I believe smoked regularly.

I do not recommend smoking at all to anyone, but especially when you are a dancer. By the time we finished a performance, I was gasping for air. Lifting as much weight as I did and break dancing continuously for as long as we did would leave most people gasping for air anyway. However, when you smoke you really feel it.

When we finally got to take a break for lunch, I was able to relax and went off to cause trouble in true Dynamic style. We were on the triangle block smack in the center of Times Square, which is where we were filming, so when the crew went to lunch they left the large cameras in place. I grabbed a clipboard and a pen and, along with my girls, stood at the very point of the triangle and pretended to passing people that I was filming a segment for this evening's news. When they were skeptical, I pointed down the block to the camera facing us. I asked each person random questions about something I can no longer recall and marked their answers on my clipboard. Each person smiled and waved at the camera, and asked what time and what channel could they see themselves on TV?

Oh, what a stinker I was. These people were home that night waiting to see themselves on TV, and probably told their family and all of their friends as well. I used to pull pranks all the time. One prank almost got us thrown in jail.

I was still with The Juice Crew, and Chino, Brian and Sammy from Incredible Breakers were hanging with us all night at The Fun House. While we were at the club, the guys were having an up-rock battle and Chino and Brian started getting really rough with each other. It looked like they would come to blows. Then one of them pulled out a switch blade and stabbed the other brother in the stomach! Clutching his stomach, the brother fell the floor (they were on the back stage) and then popped up and revealed to all who were watching that it was a trick knife! Well...

All of us decided to go to Coney Island and hang out at the beach after The Fun House, so we were all on the train headed for Brooklyn when Chino and Brian decided to have some fun and recreate their little fight scene for the benefit of two subway cars—you see, the doors connecting two cars were open, so both cars saw the scene. The brothers began their fake fight and took it between the cars. When they got in the next car, they pulled out the trick knife and one pretended to stab the other, who fell into the opened and empty conductor's booth. Needless to say, the normal passengers were horrified, but soon the victim got up, took a bow and returned to our car.

The train came to a stop in between stations, which was nothing new. So we sat and waited. The next thing we knew, several policemen came into our car and all of the passengers from the other car began pointing to us. Someone thought their little fight scene was real and they notified the police. I don't know how, because there were no cell phones back then, but there they were just the same. As we tried to explain that it was just a joke, they started searching us for weapons, which made me nervous because I did have a real switchblade on me, I always carried one back then. Well thank goodness, no one was arrested, and we all learned a lesson that day. Hey, we were over-exuberant teenagers—which means we were stupid!

As far as commercials, those were the only commercials I actually got to be in. I still get annoyed about the Mountain Dew and Pony commercials because I was duped out of doing those, but life goes on.

Although this was not a commercial, I did want to mention that The Dynamic Dolls and The Dynamic Breakers got to do something that many in the industry would have loved to have the honor that was bestowed onto us. We were invited to his studio to be photographed by the world-famous, number one photographer himself: Francesco Scavullo.

I recall arriving at his studio in Manhattan, and I was told he wanted the girls to wear black leather miniskirts. I guess mine wasn't short enough, because he had me hike it way up. I may have mentioned earlier that I always wound up doing my own makeup. However, I figured this time I would have my makeup done by a top professional. After I saw how he did Susie's makeup, I applied my own anyway. It was too retro funky for me.

It certainly wasn't what I expected, I figured we would do a few dance moves, pose, and he would take the pictures, but this was more of a fashion shoot. He had all of us oiled up from head to toe, and Susie and I were in our miniskirts with high heels. The guys were oiled up and shirtless. I have a vague memory of seeing the proofs, but I recall clearly picking up the proofs and bringing them back to our headquarters.

As I was writing this piece, I did some research online and I sent out an e-mail through Mr. Scavullo's website. He passed away some years ago. However, there are those who represent his work. I have no expectations, but who knows— maybe somewhere, those negatives or prints exist in his files. Regardless, it was still an honor and a thrill to be photographed by this legend. Francesco Suvullo was "the" photographer. When you looked at any fashion magazine, like Vogue or Cosmopolitan or Glamour, he was the one who took those photographs, on the covers as well as inside.

We also did a bunch of promotions for several of New York's top radio stations, such as WBLS Kiss FM and 92 WKTU. Those were always fun, and I liked visiting the inner workings of the radio stations. I mentioned The Dolls did a show for WBLS, but I am not sure if I told you that our very own Duce was chosen to do a campaign for WBLS, and his adorable face was plastered all over the place. Everywhere you looked, there was Duce! On the sides of buses, at every subway station and platform. I do not remember the extent of that campaign, but we were sure proud.

Then in 1985, The Dynamic Breakers did another commercial. It was an anti-graffiti ad which I believe may still be viewed on YouTube. By this time The Dolls had moved on and were no longer performing. I may have missed one or two commercials, but this is to the best of my own recollection.

Chapter 14—The Search is On

For a while The Dolls consisted of just Susie Q and me, and we searched high and low to try and find a third Doll. We would have preferred four females in our crew, but we were having such a hard time trying to find just one. To be considered, a female had to be a versatile dancer, have break dancing skills, and she had to be able to learn choreography—lots of choreography. We had auditioned several females, but none of them were even close to what we needed. In the meantime, Susie Q and I kept on working.

We were always so busy, and I always did a pretty good job of keeping a schedule of what we had lined up, but even then I did not always know what we were walking into.

For example:

Our manager, Cord, had given me an announcement for a show we had coming up. It was for a fashion show at Studio 54, where top designer Ted Lapidus was revealing his latest line. When we arrived, I noticed immediately that something was wrong. There wasn't a stage for us to perform on, but a long runway, which is expected at a fashion show. Now, we were good, I have had to perform in some pretty tight spaces at times, but how we supposed to perform on this very narrow runway? My first thought was of me spinning Susie on my head in such a narrow area.

I went to find Cord and express my concerns, when we received a pleasant surprise. We did not have to dance at all! He told us that all we had to do was escort the male models down the runway and back. Talk about a sweet job and an easy paycheck. Now, I have never modeled or walked down a runway in my life. We almost had a similar gig with designer Norma Kamali—we worked with her, she gave us the outfits we were to wear, but we never wound up doing that gig, I don't know why.

So I did what I have done my entire life when I had to do something I had never done before—play it off. Now we have all seen models walk up and down a runway in our lives, so I would just do what I had seen them do.

We were not dressed to wear Ted Lapidus tweed blazers with the patches on the elbows, but we made it work. It just so happened my mother and my sister were in the audience, and my mother told me that my sister was shocked at my performance. "Look at her, Mom, she's up there walking just like the models do," my sister said. "Oh my God, how is she doing that in front of all of these people?" My sister was not as outgoing as I was. I believe there is a certain something we all have as adolescencts where we just take things in stride. I don't know—all I know is that's how I was. I mean, with all of the amazing things we did and places we went and the people we did them with, I just took it all in stride. I never felt anyone was better than me, yet I did not feel like I was better than them, either.

So Susie and I put on the blazers, pushed up the sleeves, and we were off. We took turns escorting each gorgeous male model up and down the runway until it was all over. The easiest money we ever made. Talking about good looking guys I have to tell you the story of me and Erik Estrada.

The Dolls were invited to an after-party for some awards show. I do not know if it was the Emmys, but we put on our best and went along with our manager. We were standing by a railing overlooking a huge wall of screens that were showing highlights of the awards show and interviews from the red carpet. Directly below us on the main floor was a sunken area lined with red cushions to sit on, kind of like a sunken living room. There were railings all around it, except for the entrance. There stood a large bodyguard, and who was he guarding? Yes, Erik Estrada.

Now I was never a big fan of his. Oh, I liked the show Chips when I was a kid, but I though Erik Estrada was full of himself—and boy, was I right. Every woman in the place found their way over to his lair, and boy was he hamming it up. So me being the troublemaker that I am, I found an ashtray with wet, soggy cigarette butts in it to my left. I took one and flicked it toward Mr. Estrada. A bulls–eye, right in the middle of his back. It left a gray ash mark, Cord half-heartedly protested my childish behavior, but with my second launch and hit, he began laughing hysterically. By the time I ran out of butts, Mr. Estrada looked like a spotted leopard from behind!

In the meantime Susie introduced me to a young lady who had recognized us and wanted to know if we were interested in adding another Doll to our crew, and she asked if she could audition. I spent some time speaking with her and told her I would give her our contact information so we could set up an audition for her. Now I was just standing at the same railing with Cord when all of a sudden, who comes and stands right beside me?

At first I thought I was busted and Mr. Estrada had come to confront me, but that was not the case. I was the one woman in the entire room who had no interest in him whatsoever, so of course he approached me. I was not unpleasant, but I by no means gave him the star treatment he was looking for.

Our conversation was all about him, of course, although he did mention his co-star Larry Wilcox from Chips. Apparently Mr. Wilcox was so jealous of Mr. Estrada that he tried to copy his winning smile when they reshot the opening of Chips, and that upset him terrible. Oh, he took great care to mention that Larry Wilcox's smile could never compete with his own no matter how hard he tried, and that their relationship had faltered because of Mr. Wilcox's growing jealousy.

Oh dear Lord, give me a break. I could not have been more disinterested if I was watching paint dry, and his immense ego was too much for me to take. My manager was still standing next to me, so I said "excuse me" to Mr. Estrada and pretended to be deep in a very important conversation with Cord until Mr. Estrada was either called away or left. Whew, that was a chunk of my life I will never recover from. Here comes the best part...

I remembered to write down my information for the girl who wished to audition, and I headed off to give it to her when I noticed I'd left something out and returned to where I was standing to add it onto the business card. Behind where I was standing was a long row of steps, like in a theatre, going up to these platforms on either side. On these platforms sat tables for two with tablecloths and candles. I needed to climb the narrow, steep steps in order to hand the girl my information. It was pretty dark, so I was being very careful as I climbed the steps.

Once we finished talking, I headed back down the same steps, being just as careful. I did not want to fall and get hurt or embarrass myself, plus I had on a dress and heels. When I made it down, I headed back toward Cord who was laughing and clapping. I thought he was laughing at me and clapping because I made it without falling. He said to me, "I love it. You made him look like such a fool. That was great, I love you." I had no idea what he was talking about, and Cord seemed slightly disappointed when he realized what he thought I did on purpose was nothing but a mistake—but he still seemed thrilled with the results. Here is what happened.

As I headed cautiously up the steps with business card in hand to deliver it to that girl, I already explained to you how careful I was being, which meant I was looking down to make sure I hit each step, and occasionally I glanced up toward my destination. Apparently Erik Estrada was up in those stands and had seen me writing down what he thought was my phone number on the card. As I climbed the steps and reached his level, he walked to the end of the aisle to greet me and put his hand out to receive the card I held in my hand, assuming it was for him. When I continued and just passed him by, still standing there with his hand out, Cord said he was mortified and pulled back his hand and quickly looked around to see if anyone else had witnessed him being snubbed.

I never even saw Erik Estrada up there, either on my way up or my way down. As I said, it was dark and I was so focused on not falling. However I did enjoy Cord's version of what took place during my climb, and good for him assuming I was giving him my digits. Well, that was my little experience with Erik Estrada—and by the way, it never worked out with that girl either. Our search would have to continue...

I remember this one night Cord said we were going to a club because someone we knew—I don't remember who it was—deejayed there club and we were going to show our support, so we went. We stayed high above the dance floor in a VIP room right off the DJ booth. It was cool because we got to see the entire dance floor and all of the dancers. I do remember wanting to skip out of there ASAP. After all, we were always in clubs, and to be honest I wasn't feeling this one.

I can still see it all in my memory. It's like I am reliving it all over again in my mind. I can see me and Susie on the main floor, and we were walking through the crowded dance floor when I spotted a small circle of females. I grabbed hold of Susie's arm and led her toward them with me. There were three females in the crew, and they were wearing matching jackets with their crew's name: "Tri-Style Females." I wasn't really impressed, but then one of the girls got down and I thought she had potential. That was JaeCie. We asked her on the spot if she would be interested in trying out to possibly become a Dynamic Doll, I believe she faltered for a moment. After all, we did kind of blindside her, and in front of her own crew.

I believe I made the choice a little easier for her. I asked her if her crew was performing and making money. I asked her if her crew was on national television lately, or if they had traveled out of the country to perform. She shook her head no. Well, I told her, if you work out, these are the things you will be doing as a Dynamic Doll. JaeCie stepped over to her friends and spoke with them. She came back to me and nodded okay, and I gave her the information as to where and when we would try her out.

Her immediate skills were not the most important factor. She could always get better. We had to see if she could follow and learn the choreography. She had to pick it up quickly and she had to be on point, especially since she was not accustomed to performing in front of thousands, sometimes millions of people. Needless to say she fit the bill, and was now our third and final member of The Dynamic Dolls.

JaeCie quickly fit in—not only with the Dolls, but she also got a thumbs-up from our male counterparts, The Dynamic Breakers. JaeCie was hard working and determined and we needed a female like her, because we had plenty of gigs lined up and she had to be ready. I just got off the phone with JaeCie minutes ago. I am proud to say that we are still friends, and I love when we reminisce together. If I didn't live so far away, we would be hanging out together a lot. Unfortunately, Susie Q is doing her own thing and has no contact with any of us any longer.

Chapter 15—Regrets

In life we all have regrets, and I am no different. I have more than a few regrets when it comes to my career as a B-Girl. The first on the list actually covers several of them, and that would be I regret passing up or walking away from so many opportunities. These are the ones that top the list.

I passed up the leading role in the movie "Body Rock" because they asked me if I would be willing to do partial nudity. It's not so much that I would have said yes if given the chance again. However, I would have tried to negotiate a little bit to see if there was a way around it, or I could have been dishonest and agreed to doing nudity, and when the time came changed my mind. What could they have done at that point? The film would have been weeks, maybe months into production. They certainly could not have replaced me at that time, so maybe they would have gotten a stand-in or body double.

Then there was the movie "Beat Street." I would have paid more attention to what was going on before the auditions, but I left everything up to our managers. I could have tried to get a speaking part, but in hindsight I certainly would not have walked away from filming after the first day. Who knew the movie would become iconic after thirty years? Although what I said earlier was true, that we did have other big jobs to do, I could have made it work. Just because none of my other crew members showed up for filming was no reason for me to walk out, too.

Breakin' 2: Electric Boogaloo. Due to the lack of trust I now had for my managers, I tried to orchestrate this opportunity on my own. After all, Michael "Boogaloo Shrimp" was my friend, my contact, so who needed my manager? Maybe if I gave Cord the information, I could have had him set up an audition for me. However, he probably would have hooked up the guys instead, as he usually did. If Michael and I were not in different countries and we would have been able to reach one another in time, then I had a very good chance of being in that movie as well.

I regret that we did not have different management because all of the huge opportunities that were kept from us or sabotaged by our own management. If we had management that had our best interests at heart, I believe The Dynamic Dolls would have really taken the world by storm. My managers had something that nobody else had—like lightening in a bottle, it sold itself.

I think back to the meeting between the owners of the famous club The Roxy and The Dynamic Dolls in their office. They wanted to be our managers, but we were already under contract with other managers.

I regret that I did not do everything possible to make sure I had all of our performances that were on tape copied and in my possession. It's funny, I have written in my pink appointment book from back in those days: "*Make sure you get copies of the Morning Show with Regis and The Beat Street Strut video from Cord.*"

I think the video I would want the most is a show we did at the skating rink in Queens, which was Dynamic territory, the turf where Dynamic started. I had a popping solo and I was in my zone. No rushing through it, just me in my zone—and I remember watching the video later and it was the first time I was able to watch myself without cringing. As a matter of fact, to be perfectly honest I remember saying out loud, "Damn, I am good."

I think if you readers saw that video, you would be blown away. Remember, originally I was sought after by so many crews because of my popping skills.

I don't want to bore you with all of my regrets, so I will finish with the last one. I regret walking away from everything after Susie Q quit the Dolls because she and Kano were going to have a baby. I had so many connections, I could have gone into so many other areas, like choreography, teaching, acting, production—who knows? I had the talent and the connections. It's funny that The Dynamic Dolls could have been among some of the very first female rappers. Seriously, remember when I wrote about us recording the backgrounds for the guys' record "Total Control" at Sunnyview records?

Joe Webb from Sunnyview Records loved what I had written for The Dolls, and he loved our rapping skills. Many times after a performance (and they did this to us a few times while on tour), the announcer would get on the mike and do a little interview with us right there on the center stage after we just finished performing, so we were out of breath.

After they asked us our names and where we came from, we were supposed to each do a little rap. For instance, I usually said, "With a capital K, I'm known as Kim-A-Kazi, my moves are flame throwin', always flowing naturally. Waves go thru my body like an electrical force, I'm in a rage on the stage when it's time to go off." There is a lot more to it, but I don't think I'll embarrass myself any further. Hey, I never said was Lil' Kim!

The crowds went wild, but you know what? We were not interested, because dancing was our passion and what we loved to do. Being that music is the biggest money maker out of the five elements of Hip Hop, I do regret The Dolls not giving it a try, Oh, well.

It is ironic just how everything worked out for me. Movies, commercials, records that would have made me as big as my peers—maybe bigger. All the videos of my real skills and The Dynamic Dolls at our best lost, missing or being held hostage by those who do not want you to see them.

Think about this; If I have exaggerated about my skills and how good The Dynamic Dolls were, and we were not so good, then I would think these people would have posted those videos on YouTube a long time ago.

Like one B-Boy said to me: "In one way, these people are only adding to the mystique of the legend of The Dynamic Dolls." I understand just what he means. We can only hope that one day this foolishness will end, I would like my family to be able to see what we used to do. It is beyond me that anyone could be that cruel as to deny someone their own memories.

Speaking of memories, several times I have referred to my old pink appointment book. It went with me whereever I went, and it is chock full of history. You should see the phone numbers I have in that book, B-Boys from almost every major crew on the East Coast, and some of the big ones from the West Coast. I think Hip Hops fans would get a kick out of them. This book itself is a part of Hip Hop history, not to mention all of the appointments I have written in it. I am so glad this book remained with me.

I am lucky to have many of my memories still with me, because almost everything I had was lost. I was on tour and although I had my own place, most of my stuff was still at my mother's house. When I returned from that tour, I found my family had moved. My mother had some problems with the owners of the house, and it turned out they locked the place up with many of our possessions still inside! Everything of mine was gone by the time I got back. All of my school and class photos, all of my clothes, Webbo outfits and boots. I had like twenty pairs of those suede boots in every color.

All of my awards, trophies, most of my records and albums—just about everything I owned. Still to this day, I cannot fathom how anyone could be so greedy and mean as to actually throw out someone's memories. My graduation book that everyone signed—gone. Things that cannot be replaced and are sentimental bother me the most. Also gone were my original Swatch watches, the packs of stickers Imperials Toys sold of us, all gone. Okay, I am moving on because it still infuriates me.

A few years ago, four to be exact, I got together with a friend who is a Hip Hop enthusiast and is big on Hip Hop history, and he agreed to film and edit a documentary on The Dynamic Dolls and The Dynamic Breakers. It took some doing, but I finally managed to book a time and place for all of us to meet and film our documentary.

It wound up being Kano, Duce, Spyder, Airborne and me, of course. We had a great time and plenty of great footage. I thought it would be great if we could get a few of our friends, peers, and those we were on tour with to say a little something on our documentary. I was working it out where I was getting at least one member from each group that was on the Fresh Fest tour with us to participate. I had secured three and was working on the rest, when all of a sudden the three I thought I had secured just stopped communicating with me. No explanations, just silence, I can surmise why. However, unless I know it for a fact, I just won't touch it.

Unfortunately and despite my staying on top of him, three years had passed and this guy had never even completed our documentary. It got ugly for a while, and I retrieved our footage. I set out to find someone else to do the editing, because there is some great history, information and stories that most people have never even heard before. To be honest, after finding out that my own crew member was purposely withholding footage of The Dolls' performances, I decided to put the project aside for now.

The whole idea of doing the documentary was my idea. Originally the documentary was supposed to be about me, but as usual, I wanted to involve all of my crew members. Besides, in all that time, not one of the guys called and asked about the documentary except Duce. No one offered to help or get involved. They took no interest whatsoever. I am not sure what will become of it, but for now, I am just working hard to finish this book.

Several years ago, my friend TG called me and said he was shooting the video for Bon Rock's hit "It's Alright" featuring Keith Rodgers, and wanted me to be a part of it. He said he wanted to do a tribute to our video "The Beat Street Strut," and we began collaborating. I flew into New York and traveled to Staten Island to the location where we would be filming. It was a gray, rainy day, and unfortunately only a handful of the extras showed up.

It is not easy trying to make a crowd out of ten to twelve people. However, I told the cameraman to get a tight shot so you could not see how empty the background was. Unfortunately he didn't take direction very well. There are shots of me directing the crowd when I am not even supposed to be in the shot. The funny thing is, I was just supposed to be in the video, but old habits die hard. So when I saw that certain things were not going right, I opened my big mouth. If I had known TG a little better at that time, I would have stepped in much earlier and more often.

For instance, the people who did show up were camera shy. The setting was supposed to be a club, so I told them to relax and just act like they would when they are out partying, but it seemed like no one wanted to put themselves out there first. We went downstairs to shoot the scene where I help the girl by teaching her a few quick B-Girl moves, and I then change her appearance from nerd girl to Fly B-Girl. We then head upstairs to rejoin the party, where she busts it out, ultimately getting her man.

By the time we finished filming and headed back upstairs, the extras had relaxed and gotten to know one another, so when we started filming again they were ready to go. It was a lot of fun—and of course, when I first got there I still got the "Who is this white girl and what's she gonna do?" But by the time we were done, those same females were real cool. I even got hugs and kisses good-bye. Pretty cool.

When we were filming the part where I teach the girl how to dance, people got to see what bad shape I am really in. While trying to do up-rock, a simple move, the muscle knots I have all over my entire body were getting stuck behind my knee cap, causing my leg to collapse out from under me. I think you can see it in the video. Then when I had to do simple footwork on the floor, I had two braces on my left wrist (that was the wrist I injured during the show for Liza Minnelli and Chita Rivera), but I still could not support any weight on it, so I kept falling. Ha! Some B-Girl.

Just after we wrapped, Bon Rock was still jamming and more people had joined us. Everyone was hanging out and talking when I heard someone shouting something about another legend up in here. I looked around to see who had come in, when I saw this guy heading straight for me, saying, "Oh man, I have got to meet you and shake your hand!"

"Why didn't anyone tell me she was here? I got to get a picture with this legend," he said, and he kept going on and on. I said to him, "Are you sure you aren't confusing me with someone else?" I asked him several times, but he knew who I was. He was like, "Uou used to be spinning those dudes on your head, and your poppin' was crazy." Talk about getting a compliment!

We took a bunch of photos, but I kept closing my eyes. I couldn't help it—my illness makes me sensitive to sound, light and odors, so when someone uses a camera that flashes twice, I close my eyes. Anyway, he asked for my digits as well. When I found out who this guy was, I was so embarrassed, and I asked again if I wasn't being confused with someone else. TG told me he was Tiger from the Wu-Tang Clan! Now, I do not know every member of the Wu-Tang Clan, but I should have been the one asking him for some photographs—for real.

I also was a guest on "The Old School Radio Hour" and I had a blast. When I first walked in I got the usual reaction from the females, but after a short time they were real cool with me. I got to see my old friend Fastbreak from Magnificent Force, and Tony Tone from the legendary Cold Crush Brothers was there too. I have to tell you, me and Tony was snapping on one another and we laughed our asses off! So much of the interview had to be cut because of the laughing and the naughty things we were saying. A day I will always remember fondly.

I recently was invited by Shabba-Doo to be interviewed on his new Internet radio spot, "Breakin' News with Shabba-Doo." Besides me, Tony "Mr. Wave" was on as well. Mr. Freeze was supposed to be on too, but he asked to be removed just days before, I do not know why. It worked out better without him, if you ask me, because when there are too many personalities at once it can get a little crazy. I think Shabba-Doo does a great job as host. He keeps things flowing. I really enjoyed the experience.

Left: TG – Kim-A-Kazi – Fastbreak @ The Old School Radio Hour

Chapter 16—Where Are They Now?

I, **Kim-A-Kazi**, along with my husband and son, moved from Brooklyn, New York to Las Vegas, Nevada, in the year 1999. I love living here, except for the fact that my friends and family are so far away. I also miss out on many opportunities back in New York because I am not in the thick of things. Due to my many injuries and severe fibromyalgia, along with a host of other issues, I was forced to stop working years ago. You try explaining to the doctors that the reason your neck bone is bent backwards and crushed against your brainstem is because when you were a teenager, you used to put people on your head and spin them with no hands. Then when they get a look at your spine and the rest of you...well, I find showing a photo saves me a lot of time and explanations.

The funny thing is that so many people throughout my life have no idea that I was an original B-Girl. It's just not something I went around telling everyone. When social media came around and people I had never heard of started contacting me, it was beyond me how they knew who I was. Social media has been a blessing to me, because I have had so many amazing people reach out to me. I choose the people I accept on Facebook carefully. To me it's not about the quantity, but the quality, and I am blessed by all of the wonderful friends I have. Many started out as fans and are now friends. I always accept people who are into Hip Hop and those with fibromyalgia.

For any dancer, it is a terrible thing to know that you will never be able to dance the way you love to, ever again. As a human being, it is just as devastating to accept that you will no longer be the person you always were. To someone like me, who was always active, healthy and strong, it took a very long time and a lot of suffering before I would accept that I just could not do all of the things I once did. You need to mourn the loss of who you used to be and begin to accept who you have to be now.

My condition continues to worsen and probably always will. Every single day is a struggle. From the moment I open my eyes, all I feel is terrible pain. I even moan, whimper and cry in my sleep from the pain. I haven't given up yet! I just keep the faith and hope for the best.

I can now focus on finishing all of the other books I have in the works. No more autobiographies—my passion is writing novels I also write children's stories, pre-teens, teens and adults, in all genres. I just found out through updated tests that my neck bone is actually crushed up against my brainstem, and I can't begin to realize the effects that has on my mind and body. I have trouble with brain functions, which definitely affects my writing abilities and causes me to make simple mistakes.

I will share with you a small example of how my brain and thought process is affected. I was going through my photographs for this book, and I was holding one with me wearing a black shirt with the Hip Hop Tour on the front and all the groups on the back. I have a photo of both the front and the back of the shirt, so when I finished looking at the photo of the front of the shirt, I wanted to see the back of the shirt. Instead of shuffling to the next photograph I was holding, I turned the picture over!

This may not seem like a big deal, and it is funny, but it scares me because if I have been going through memory loss for years with things I have known my entire life, and I sometimes have trouble knowing what year it is right off the bat, then what will I be like in a few more years? That is very scary. Yes, I know as we age, we lose memories, and we cannot do things as we once did. But this is a whole different ballgame. I could write a whole other book on all of the experiences I have had because of my illnesses and my injuries. Some are funny, many are not.

I am not complaining, just explaining—so once again I am faced with obstacles that I must deal with in order to achieve my dreams. Like dancing, writing and being

164

creative came very naturally to me. To write should be a happy, pleasant event, but now I have to write with a severe handicap. And although I will not let it stop me, I get angry, for it is just one more thing that this illness has ruined for me. I may get pushed down, but I always get back up.

On a more positive note, there are still so many things I would like to do. I hope I will get the opportunity to do as many as I can.

As far as all my other crew members, JaeCie works for a law firm and is a promoter for many clubs and hot spots in the NYC area. JaeCie also rides a motorcycle and is part of an all-female motorcycle crew—keeping with tradition.

Duce has carved out an impressive career in the music world. DJ, MC, music producer—the list goes on. His resume is impressive, and he is sought after all over the world and travels extensively. Duce has worked with many celebrities, producing their music. He is always the life of the party and one of the friendliest guys you can meet.

Kano has one of the most impressive lives. He served in the Army while raising his two children into wonderful, successful adults. Just this year he came for a visit with his son, who is also serving in the Army. Kano does missionary work and travels to other countries to build churches, orphanages, schools and other facilities for underprivileged people.

Kano runs a successful business and is a proud grandpa. I doubt I am representing him to his fullest potential, for he has accomplished so much in his life, but he remains a very close friend—no, more than that, family. I treasure our thirty-three year relationship.

As for the rest of our crew, some have stayed in the entertainment business and others have gone a different way. None have shown much interest in trying to get into the spotlight again as many others are doing, and I understand that, because as I have said many times over, what we accomplished was out of a passion for dancing, not to obtain fame. I do, however, want all of Dynamic to get the acknowledgement that we deserve.

If I had a dime for every person who has told me that it was because of The Dynamic Rockers, Breakers and Dolls that they started breaking, or told me they would watch us perform and then copy all of our moves, I'd have a nice little bankroll. I know there are many people out there who are thrilled that Dynamic has not tried to claim their rightful place alongside all of others who are trying to gain fame, and even immortality out there, and they will do whatever it takes to get a foothold on such a platform.

I am not unlike some of these people in a way. I would like The Dynamic Dolls to be recognized for all of our achievements and the barriers that we broke down, especially since there are so many who want to keep us from doing so. However, I am not interested in lying or sucking up to anyone to do so. I wrote this book mainly because so many people wanted me to. When I would share a few stories with them, they insisted I write a book, and so I did. I feel our history is important. As I have said, there can only be one first, and The Dynamic Dolls were it. Besides, I had to write this before I forget it all.

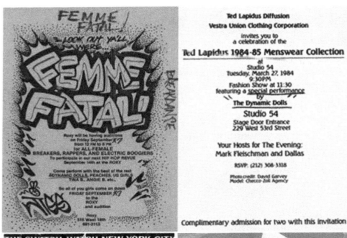

Flyers from my personal collection

Note: Femme Fatal flyer (They were referring to Peaches the singer)

In Conclusion

Well, ladies and gentlemen, we have come to the end of my journey thus far.

Our contributions in the art of break dancing are legendary. Our moves and choreography are still being used today and are staples for any B-Boy or B-Girl learning how to break dance. The Dynamic Dolls were not some fly-by-night crew. Our routines, skills and showmanship were unmatched 33 years ago, but we would still be a force to be reckoned with, even today. Don't get me wrong—the moves today's B-Girls have on the floor are incredible. However, as far as a crew, routines and my lifting skills, we are still unmatched.

I believe it is important for B-Girls to know that they too have a history, and it begins with The Dynamic Dolls. There may have been other females that hung out on the corner or in the school yard and who did a little up-rock or some basic footwork, but The Dynamic Dolls broke through all the barriers, becoming the first and the best professional female break dance crew. And I support all B-Girls far and wide, and will do whatever I can to help B-Girls receive equal treatment and billing as the B-Boys.

Most importantly, I hope you enjoyed taking this journey down memory lane with me. I hope there were times you almost felt as if you were there with us. If I made you chuckle just once, and maybe brought you some new information you had never heard before, then I am happy.

I want to thank you for your support, and I would like to wish you all the very best on your own journeys through life. When you do something, give it your all. Always try to do the right thing—trust me, karma will reward you. *Never give up or get down on yourself if things do not go the way you hoped. You never know which doors were closed to you so you could go through the doors you were meant to.*

For all of you dancers, I remind you to be careful and never rush by doing a move you have not perfected. Remember, it is better to lose a battle orcompetition than to lose the ability to dance again tomorrow. I have told you how I live with the pain of my mistakes, pushing myself to the extreme and not wanting to miss out on any performance. I know many dancers do the same thing, and though we do get hurt along the way, doing a move you have not perfected in the heat of a battle can be dangerous, even deadly.

Although my heart aches because I can never do all of the things I used to do as far as dancing, flips, flying!, I always enjoy watching others, and I am still stunned by the amazing moves today's B-Boys and B-Girls are executing.

You all rock!

Chapter 17—Testimonials

It is not so much the fact that more people backed out of writing their testimonials for this book than those who actually did. What is more important, and what means more to me, are those who did take the time to write something without fear of ridicule or choosing "sides." Just the fact that they did means more to me than any compliments paid me. So I want to thank them from the bottom of my heart. I also want to give props to those involved in Hip Hop who were told not to deal with me or even speak to me, and who did not comply. I know nobody could tell me who I could speak to or not.

I wanted to have a graffiti piece made on the back of my jacket. Twelve artists later and I still have no piece. I have been referred to each one, and every one of them I had a great connection with, and then something started happening with some of them. All of a sudden, nothing. I heard nothing from them again. Each time this happened I looked at their Facebook page, and they all had one specific connection. The ones who remain friends with me out in the open, despite what they had been told, are the only ones I have an interest in knowing anyway. Imagine at our age, such childish behavior exists. I have much respect for those certain people (they know who they are) who saw the real me and went against the masses. Thanks to all of you!

Jerri Council:

"I've known Kim for three decades. Did you know that before she became a mom, wife, crafter, or a self-published author (during the foundation of HIP-HOP back in the 1980s), Kim was the hardest working B-Girl in the renowned Hip-Hop dance troop, THE DYNAMIC DOLLS!? My girl's footwork was perfection, the precision of her Tuts were flawless, and her ability to SPIN A MAN ON HER HEAD has NEVER been matched!

Kim-A-Kazi Valente

Can you say, "AMAZING"? Kim's talent has been applauded nationally and internationally in clubs, theaters, and arenas.

Her visage has plugged products in teen idol magazines, and in commercials (forgive me; I failed to mention her beauty–inside and out). And, she was cheered for her talents on the BIG and small screen, where her skills were showcased in a hit movie, and the most popular TV shows of that era.

In my opinion, KIM VALENTE a.k.a. KIM-A-KAZI is HIP-HOP ROYALTY...All hail THE QUEEN!"

~Jerri Council ~

Author–Memoirs of a Forgotten Success Story; Artist; Creative Director; Momager to Icon Shaik a.k.a. Little Shake; Style Enthusiast.

George Lumpkins:

I was born and raised in Boston, MA. During my teen years, 1980-86, Boston caught the break dance bug. I was hooked from the start. I actually learned from a really good group of guys from Providence, R.I. They used to rock at a skate rink called The U.S.A. I can remember from seeing my first windmill, to hand spin to backspin, I was hooked and wanted to learn.

I didn't get a chance to visit often, so I tried to learn all I could in one weekend. I had managed to learn just enough to get me back to Boston to get a group of my friends together, to show them what I had learned over the weekend. Looking back on it, with the lack in technology, this was a big deal. I had very basic top rock (no style), just arm movements back and forth, 6-step footwork, which was more like running around in a circle, and floats, crab-walk, jackhammers (all the same move, but depending where you are from, called a different name).

Eventually we formed a group that went through two names to get it right. The first name was the Heart-Breakers. We thought it would be cool with the girls. It lasted through one school talent show, so we named ourselves The Boston City Breakers.

At that time all we had was each other and whatever movie we could watch. Style Wars, Wild Style, Beat Street, and that one episode of Graffiti Rock. The one thing we had heard but never got a chance to see was the famous Lincoln Center Battle with Rock Steady vs. Dynamic. Word of this battle was getting all around, and eventually we got to see some small clips. During this time, Hip-Hop was growing and there was a tour headlined by Run-DMC, Whodini, (UTFO was the B-Boys backing them up) The Fat Boys, Kurtis Blow and the Dynamic Breakers. It was called The Fresh Fest. This was the first Hip-Hop Tour. It was filled with all the rappers/emcees we were listening to at the time.

We had to take a 45 minute bus ride to Providence, R.I. When we got to the show, we knew of some of the rap acts, but what we really wanted to see was *Dynamic*. We had heard so much about them and were at the front of the stage. On the stage, we just remember seeing this nonstop show of action. It was the Dynamic Breakers. At the time we didn't know who we were looking at, because we never saw Dynamic perform.

From what I can remember, Jermaine Dupri came out first. He must have been about 8 or 9 years old. He had popping moves, pretty basic with some glides, but nothing on the level of some of the boogie boys we knew at the time. What we really enjoyed about Dynamic's performance was it was like a circus filled with flips, spins and very fast windmills.

One of the most *mind blowing things* we had never seen before was the 2- and 3-person tabletops. No other crew was spinning anyone on top of their heads, and yet we remember saying, *Oh sh%t, that's a girl, spinning that dude!?* Honestly, I'm pretty sure we said, *damn, that's a strong-ass white girl.* Now the only time we saw a girl rocking was Baby-Love doing basic footwork in Beat Street. Our girls in Boston we more about popping and waving and not interested in breaking.

172

We thought oh, damn, they brought the heat with this show. I remember looking at the fliers from the show and seeing names like Airborne, Duce, Spider, Flip and Kano. I wish I still had the flier, because it had pictures and everything.

I remember there was a separate performance in which there were a few young ladies that were also rocking. At that time most folks were walking around, talking to people and buying stuff. But I and my crew stayed to watch the performance. I remember being impressed to see you and the Dolls rocking. I didn't know who was whom at the time, but remember being impressed by the popping routines and the girl with the back spin.

As I am writing this, I'm gonna assume you were the "spinner" because there was no Kim-A-Kazi back then, Wow. amazing how the memory works when you get into a creative writing flow. *We actually borrowed a lot of moves from Dynamic and incorporated them into our shows.* We did more flips, added the tabletop and actually upgraded the 3-person hurricane/tabletop and added two people on the wings and called it the 5-man tornado. Corny names, but yeah we borrowed a lot of the fast flip and spin moves from Dynamic and you. Thank you. I guess we owe you residual fees for copyrighted moves.

There are bits and pieces I do remember more of Dynamic, like the appearance on 'That's Incredible," and there was a show that was on the news that made headlines. I think it was called the "Big Break" dance contest. I remember there were a bunch of crews and they were being judged by ex-football player Herschel Walker. The other piece I remember about you was being in the Beat Street Strut Video with the Dolls. Doing the 3-person hurricane/tabletop, the dive and roll into the headache, classic B-Boy/B-Girl moves.

(Note: I actually was using the name Kim-A-Kazi, even before the Fresh Fest tour)

A **B-Girl** in a B-Boy World

From OSJ:

Much Love, Kim...I was just reading some comments on the Beat Street Strut video on YouTube. That was intense how the newbies don't know their Hip Hop history. You did an awesome job putting their facts right with a bit of swearing, which of course made you very angry. But I must take my hat off to you for making us understand how things could've been a whole lot different then..."Respect."

To those who haven't read her comments, you should.

Samantha Allende– Sister to Susie Q:

Put this in your book, Sis...there is no other B-Girl like Kim-A-Kazi...you are the best of the best. You inspired me to dance myself, and I remember thinking about you before my dance recitals and saying to myself that I was going to put my "Kim All" into my performance.

I was Baby Dynamic Doll at heart and could kick myself for being too shy to dance in front of you when I was a little girl! You danced with your heart and soul...and I pray for a miracle, so that I can see you dance again!

Richard "Fastbreak" Williams:

(a comment written on Facebook–March 27, 2015)

Hold up, wait a minute! Let's not forget the Dynamic Dolls, who were *the only* B-Girl crew of girls who were catching wreak as well and getting the attention within, competing amongst the guys on the dance floor.

Yes, Kim-A-Kazi, you did held it down for the (LADIES), with Susie Q and etc. your HISTORY too as WELL. (NO OTHER, FEMALE CREWS we're holding it DOWN.) Yes, these girls can REALLY DANCE.

I always remember Kim, when it came to dancing a lot of guys was afraid to go up against you girls because you knew how to out dance them. It was egos and reps on the line, especially if you had a name out there... Your brother, FastBreak. Stay beautiful and blessed.

Note: Now here is a wonderful man and a secure one who is not afraid to tell it like it is, no matter who may not like it, and I give him much respect and love. We go way back and we have done a few projects together, like The Old School Radio Hour and the Bon Rock video.

Nicholas wrote: "I have to give Kim-A-Kazi Valente a LOT of CREDIT for this move: the 3-Man Helicopter and the 2-Man Helicopter. Very difficult & very dangerous move ! Romeo & I did these same MOVES. But I learned how to do it correctly by watching Kim at the FUNHOUSE! Thank you. Kim!"

On The Down Low:

People told me I should take some of the things that people say to me on the QT, so I have posted just a few of them. The names have been left out, because I am not looking to call anyone out. It is a shame so many people, for whatever their reasons, won't speak out loud. They will only write to me in my "inbox" where nobody else can see. Some, however, were written with love and kindness as part of a conversation. P,S, They have not been edited in anyway. As you read them is exactly how they were written to me.

I have many more, but I just wanted to share a few with you. I do give credit to those, however, who are not afraid to speak out loud—not only about The Dynamic Dolls, but about all of Dynamic.

From "D.L.":

You are like a star to me, just like people who meet movie stars! I would rather meet you in person than any movie star! That is the truth!!One always! Thank you for messaging me!!I feel so special! Lol!!

I am 100% truthful when I say I would rather meet you than a movie star! I am so honored to have you message with me! I feel like I've won a contest! Lol!! You seem very humble, but please tell your story like it is! We all know you are a top dancer, never mind being a female! It ain't braggin' if it's true! I love the tidbits of info you tell me! It's like a sneak preview of block buster movie you've been dying to see for a year!!Some many great stories! I love it!!!!

From–M.C.:

I posted your video "The Beat Street Strut" because I was doing a project about old school Hip Hop and do you know what people posted? Nothing!

No one would say anything because they know they can't say anything bad about you or your crew. So they say nothing! It is so sad that this is how you and your crew are treated and why? Because of hate? Don't worry I always got your back!

From–D.E.:

I was a dancer at The Fun House too but I was nowhere even close to the Amazing dancer that Kim was. When I used to see her at The Fun House way before breaking took over Kim was even a great dancer then. I'll never forget this amazingly insane spin Kim used to do. She looked like a tornado! I wanted to lean how she did that spin and she showed me. Over and over again but I just couldn't get it. We lived right near one another and sometimes we took the train home together. As the style of dance changed and Kim started popping and breaking, I didn't see her much after that but I couldn't believe how good she became and how fast too.

I always thought I was a good dancer but if I lived a hundred years I could never become half the dancer Kim was. I mean to lift human beings up in the air and spin around like they were nothing! I was lucky I could give my little brother a piggy back ride lol.

The reason I only used my initials is because there are certain people I am friends with that would be furious if they knew I wrote this for Kim. It is true what Kim says, there are people who are mean and who would not speak one kind word about Kim simply because they were jealous of her. I was jealous of Kim back then but not in a bad or mean way. I just wished I could dance like she did. Kim would show anyone who asked how to do a move of hers she just loved to dance and wasn't ever stuck up no matter how big she got. But more importantly she is such a nice person and I am so happy we reconnected after so many years.

I am glad Kim is finally telling her story. I can't wait to get a copy of her book.

Kano (Milton Torres) The Dynamic Breakers:

I know talent when I see it and I do not have a problem giving props to those who deserve it. All I know is this: I fell right into the hip hop culture just when it was in its infancy, I have seen many talented B-boys as well as a ton of wanna be' but when it came to B-Girls, well let's face it, there were barely none. With that being said, I honestly can't say *"I have never met or seen any other B-girl that had the skill level that you had"*.

You were *a free stylist, up rocker, breaker and a popper*. Out of all those, I remember you most for your popping. I mean yeah you were *strong as shit* and saved *our tour at Fresh Fest*, but there was something about how *you hit* them pops and locks (too fresh as Cord would say). If I were to rank B-girls of that era, and those who ran in the circuit, I would honestly have to say **you were #1** on the list because of your versatility. Not too many people can claim that. Make no doubt Kim-A-Kazi you were dope. And I am not blowing smoke that is my honest opinion of what I know from that era.

During all this period overshadowed by the spotlight on The Dynamic Breakers, were the Dynamic Dolls; a group of all female B-Girls, led by "Kim-A-Kazi" Valente, a named given to her by me "Kano". Kim was the most predominant B-Girl during that time. She was the most forefront and pioneer of female breakers/poppers. Kim-A-Kazi was so good that she even filled in for Flip at time during his injuries. I called her Shera! The badest woman on the planet!

Kim-A-Kazi and the rest of the Dynamic Dolls have never received their well-deserved recognition in the history of Breakdancing, I would like to see that rectified.

"KANO"–"The Dynamic Breakers"

Note: In all fairness, the testimonial you just read by Kano was not actually his testimonial. This was written in an e-mail between the two of us, where I had asked Kano if he would write a little something for my book. This was part of his response to me saying that he would be happy to. I felt that his honesty and passion for how he felt was right there in the e-mail, and no other testimonial was needed. It was perfect because I did not want it to be thought about too much, or made to sound professional, or even blown up (although Kano would never do that).

Therefore I decided to use what Kano had written to me in his e-mail. It was real, true and from the heart, and what more could I ask for? On the following pages, Kano gives us an inside scoop on some important facts in Hip Hop history.

#1. You and I know that Dynamic was responsible for creating many of the moves that are still executed today and have become staple moves in break dancing, especially the original routines that you and Flip created. How do you feel about B-Boys who are trying to take credit for creating such moves as "Windmills and hand-glides when many OGs know they are lying, and even worse, they are becoming part of Hip Hop history! For example, Crazy Legs is saying he created windmills, and on {Wikipedia.}... How do you feel about this issue?

Answer: It is really sad when someone begins to claim something they had nothing to do with. Unfortunately if they are not challenged when making the claim, and whoever is doing the interview does not do any research, who is to know what is fact and what is fiction?

The proof is in the evidence. When did Crazy Legs begin doing windmills? It sure wasn't during Flashdance, or else it would have been portrayed in the movie. CL was known for his Turtle move and his wobbly legs when he floor rocked, and that's about it. More proof that he did not invent the move—most of those power moves derived from gymnastics. None of the original Rock Steady members were gymnasts. Dynamic, on the other hand, had several members who were part of their HS gymnastics teams.

It would be nice for someone to take the time to make a *real* documentary called "Break Dancing: a Hip Hop Phenomena" or something of that sort. They should research and interview all parties involved in that time period. LL Cool J knew about us even before he became famous, and so did Grandmaster Flash, whom we performed with at the Ritz way before the Big Break Dance contest.

You have That's Incredible part one with Dynamic and Rock Steady, and in part two they *only* wanted Dynamic. The information that is out there in the media is all distorted. There is a splice here, a splice there, and then there are those who should not have even been interviewed, since they were not even in the scene until afterwards.

#2. If someone asked, "What was the big deal about The Dynamic Dolls? They are just girls..." How would you respond?

Answer: That is exactly the point—they were just girls, who were just as good as, if not better than, some of the crews that were out there back in the '80s. They were minorities in a Hip Hop world dominated by all boys' crews. Salt-N-Pepa was just becoming popular in the Hip Hop scene back then, and the Dynamic Dolls were already an established and buyable group by 1984. So to me, they are a big deal, since I believe they were the first ever all-female break dancing crew.

#3. You were the only one who ever went along with me to check out the places where we were set to perform before the show. What other ways do you feel that you contributed to the success of your crew?

Answer: I am a bit humble, but to me, many of the moves that I was part of originating came from mostly karate movies that we went to see back on 42nd Street, when you could see three movies for the price of $3.50. We then went back to the studio and brainstormed how to apply some of the moves we'd seen and how to incorporate them into our routines.

The styles we wore, to me, were derived more out of necessity because of the budget that I was on back then as a starving artist. I took my old shell Adidas and, once they were worn out, I would paint them different colors. The same applied for the Pumas and the Nike Cortez. The Huevo (webbo) pants with the laces around the calves were also taken from the karate movies. Our graffiti uniforms that we won the Big Break Dance Contest with were created by neighbor who lived in the housing project next to me.

#4. What would you like the readers to know about you and your crew?

Answer: We were definitely pioneers during the infancy of the break dance era, which hit its peak between 1982 and 1986. We originated organized break dancing and brought routines to the forefront. In the beginning it was always a one-on-one battle, then Flip and I began with a duo routine. After that we began doing a lot of choreographed routines as a group, and many of the other crews followed suit. We called those groups biters, because they were copying our style.

#5. If you could go back and change anything from your dancing career, what would you change, and why?

Answer: Although we began incorporating other dance techniques into our routines—like one time we had hired a professional ballerina to do a skid to a Mozart symphony, and another time we were practicing with the original cast of *Cats*—I personally would have liked to see some of the break-dance moves incorporated into the mainstream dance arena, such as jazz, modern dance and ballet. So if I were to go back, I would have been more proactive in voicing my opinion on the matter.

#6. What, if anything, do you think the readers should know about me, Kim-A-Kazi?

Answer: I believe that given the circumstances at the time, when all focus was mainly emphasized on male-dominated break dance groups, Kim-A-Kazi and the rest of the Dynamic Dolls were overshadowed and overlooked by the mainstream media. The moves and routines that you guys had were either as good as or better than any of the other male groups at the time.

Kim-A-Kazi doing Tuts / Dolls performing @ Great Adventure

Kim-A-Kazi & Coco Pop — turn around / Kim-A-Kazi in Martinique dressing room.

Historic Tee Shirts–Kim with Mug & Official Dynamic Breakers shirt

Official Historical "Fun House Tank Top"

The First Hip Hop Tour of its Kind–The Swatch Watch Fresh Fest Tour

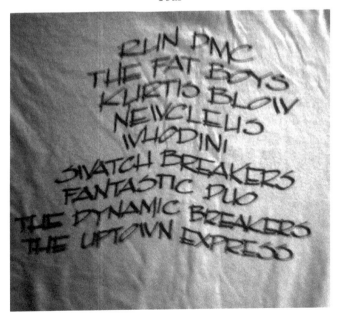

My "Juice Crew" shirt with Spinner on the front; 1982

Shirt made for the Dolls for a performance we did with the NYC Breakers

DYNAMIC
DOLLS

BREAKDANCE INTERNATIONAL
212-496-6762 · 212-679-9505 · CORD...212-

See the difference in the size and font of The Dynamic Dolls vs.
Dynamic Breakers?

Nick Abreu on the dance floor / Nick & B-Boy Romeo (Fun House Reunion). Photos by Nick Abreu.

Tiny–Richie Rock–Pablo (RIP)–Louie / Richie Rock and Pablo @The Roxy

Postcard promoting break dance lessons from the iconic Dynamic Breakers.

*This is a historic photo. I will do my best to name everybody,
starting from top row:*

*L-Wavy Legs (TDR), Samantha (TDD), Spinner (TDR),
Gloria-Mousey (RW), Kim- A-Kazi (TDD)*

Middle row right: Frank Vega & the Rockwell Crew.

*Bottom from left: Float Fastbreak (MF) and Kid Freeze —We
had performed on stage at the Puerto Rican Parade.*

Photo by Frank Vega

W.D.2. BLOW

ARTIST ENGAGEMENT CONTRACT

AGREEMENT made this   day of September, 1984 between DYNAMIC BREAKERS ("Artist") c/o Norby Walters Associates, Inc., 1650 Broadway, Suite 1410, New York, New York 10019, on the one hand, and C.W. ASSOCIATES, 5762 Deerfield Trail, College Park, Georgia 30149 and FESTIVAL VENTURES, INC., 905 Crandon Boulevard, Key Biscayne, Florida 33149, on the other, hereinafter collectively referred to as ("Purchaser").

1. Place, Date and Hours of Engagements:

The Purchaser hereby engages the Artist and Artist hereby agrees to perform the engagements set forth below (collectively referred to as the "Tour"). LOCATIONS ARE SUBJECT TO CHANGE 7 DAYS IN FRONT OF DATES.

Place	Date	Hour
1) Cincinnati, Ohio Riverfront Stadium	10/05/84	1 show - 8:00 P.M.
2) Detroit, Michigan Cobo Arena	10/06/84	1 show - 8:00 P.M.
3) Cleveland, Ohio Convention Center Arena	10/07/84	1 show - 8:00 P.M.
4) Columbia, S.C. Carolina Coliseum	10/12/84	1 show - 8:00 P.M.
5) Hampton, Virginia Hampton Coliseum	10/13/84	1 show - 8:00 P.M.
6) Philadelphia, Pa. Philadelphia Spectrum	10/14/84	1 show - 8:00 P.M.
7) St. Louis, Mo. Checkerdome Arena	10/19/84	1 show - 8:00 P.M.
8) To be determined by mutual consent		1 show - 8:00 P.M.

189

9) Memphis, Tennessee   10/21/84   1 show - 8:00 P.M.
   Mid-South Coliseum

10) Richmond, Va.   10/26/84   1 show - 8:00 P.M.
    Richmond Coliseum

11) Savannah, Georgia   10/27/84   1 show - 8:00 P.M.
    Civic Center Arena

12) Charlotte, N.C.   10/28/84   1 show - 8:00 P.M.
    Charlotte Coliseum

13) To be determined by   11/02/84   1 show - 8:00 P.M.
    mutual consent

14) Houston, Texas   11/03/84   1 show - 8:00 P.M.
    Hofheinz Pavillion

15) Dallas, Texas   11/04/84   1 show - 8:00 P.M.
    Reunion Arena

2. Rehearsal/Sound and Lights/Production:

Cities and states we were scheduled to perform while I was on the
Fresh Fest tour.

The Dynamic Breakers with Penny Marshall on "The New Show"
Cable TV 1984

Kim-A-Kazi, Spyder, Airborne, Duce and Kano – Dynamic while
filming our documentary

Third manager Terri Noel with Joe Webb from Sunnyview Records
— mentioned in Chapter 8

(L) Duce, Kim-A-Kazi, Spyder (Dynamic) & Loose Joint @ theater
in Harlem 2013 after a special showing of the original Big Break
Dance Contest @ The Roxy 83

This photo was taken after one of our performances; we're at one of our manager's apartments in Manhattan. Terri the one in the photo on the previous page.

From Top Left: Mary (Susie's mom), our two bodyguards, Susie Q

Middle Left: Coco Pop, Kim-A-Kazi, Airborne

I think the other guys were the Dynamic Three from Total Control Records

Top: Joe Flash, Shalimar, Steve from Mag Force during '84 Fresh Fest Tour

Magnificent Force & Uptown Express members and Doll JaeCie – our tour bus

Duce (L) is such a cool guy. Everyone likes him. Dynamic & Rock Steady together? Photo from Duce Martinez

*Dynamic Breakers and Dolls on our tour bus with Magnificent
Force; Swatch Watch Fresh Fest '84*

We had a lot of fun on this tour bus. We played poker
and blackjack, and we must have watched Eddie Murphy's
"Delirious" twenty times after I purchased it at some rinky-
dink video store in the middle of nowhere. It may have been
a little rinky-ink store, but they charged me like seventy to
eighty bucks for that video! Keep in mind this was 1984, and
buying a new video was expensive to begin with.

I didn't care. I had to have it, because I got tired of
listening to everyone else on the bus recite lines from the
video and laugh, yet I had no idea what they were talking
about. After just one time, I was hooked! That still is a great
standup routine and always will be.

If you happen to be one of the few who has never seen
it, you must watch it today!

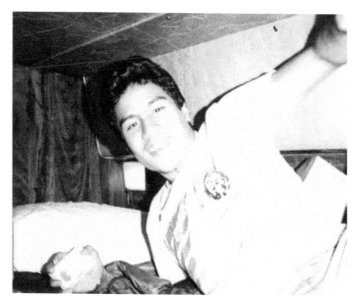

Duce in our tour bus 1984

The Dolls with manager, Upstate New York

Duce Martinez; photo by Duce Martinez   *My son, David Perelez*

David Perelez   *Shake;* photo by Shake

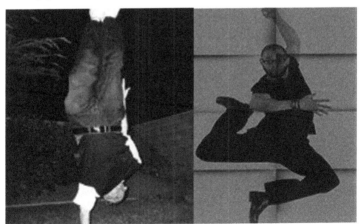

\ **Freeze** /

197

The Dynamic Dolls @ Chams DE baron after our live performance on The Morning Show with Regis Philbin; June 27th 1984, wearing outfits custom made for the Dolls (Notice mine is pink? So were the pants I was wearing.)

Bottom *—The view from the balcony in Martinique, where we got caught taking food to our room.*

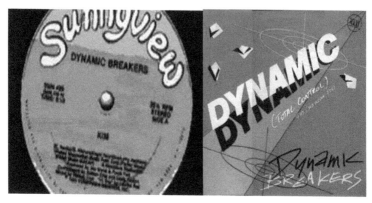

Top: "Kim" and "Total Control"; The Dynamic Breakers

*Bottom: Record given to me by Herbie Hancock @ The Fun House -
Stamped in gold: For Professional Use Only*

My Jimmy Spicer album: Wish I had my "Super Rhymes" album. Who would have thought that I would ever be friends with Jimmy? The Adventures of Super Rhymes is one of my favorite rap songs ever!

Video Burnout was handed to me outside the studio where it was recorded.

Historic business cards from my appointment book

Above: George Lumpkins, whose wrote a very informative testimonial.

Below: Dolls stickers; original Dynamic Dolls tee shirt

(L) Kim-A-Kazi '99 / (R) Our Wedding 1999, Louis & Kim

Article on The Dynamic Breakers after winning the first Big Break Dance Contest – **below:** *Dynamic/Dolls signing autographs in Italy after performances.*

Top: (L) Kim-A-Kazi / (R) Kim-A-Kazi & JaiCie @ Headquarters, Breakdance International

Bottom: (L) JaeCie doing head spins / ® Kim-A-Kazi @ Washington Kennedy Center Honors. Rhe reason I posed for this photo is because I took pictures of each Doll as they came out of the bathroom half-naked. Fair is fair, I guess. No, I don't have those pics, but I wish I still had the Beat Street tee shirt I'm wearing.

We wore florescent colored pens around our necks to sign autographs

Show Time in Italy – Kim-A-Kazi, Susie Q & The Dynamic Breakers

(L) Having photos taken for a newspaper
(R) A moment to relax during our second visit to Italy

Duce with a reporter covering the 1984 Fresh Fest tour. I swear he looks like Andy Dick. I wonder if it was Kid Freeze and Spinner a few years back.

Photo by Spinner

*Top: During the filming of our Panasonic commercial, Peter Allen
was kind enough to sign his autograph for my mom*

1st Class – Night club in Da Bronx

*This goes with the story of when we were arrested while taking lil'
Shake and his friends on an audition! I still have it.*

DYNAMIC DOLLS CREDITS

SPECIAL EVENTS:

NEW YORK MENSWEAR SHOW: New York Coliseum March 25, 1984

"JAZZTIME '84" with Chaka Khan BEACON THEATRE March 17, 1984

JVC CORPORATION Press Conference Pierre Hotel March 6, 1984

"PEPSI COLA CO. INDUSTRIAL SHOW" with Michael Jackson
              Lincoln Center N.Y. State Theatre Feb. 26, 1984

OLBIA SARDEGNA, ITALY

              Opened the Summer Music and Dance Festival Feb. 23, 1984

TWIN CITY ROLLER RINK Washington's Birthday Show
                        Elizabeth, N.J. Feb. 19, 1984

"THE RINK" CAST PARTY W/CHITA RIVERA AND LIZA MINELLI
            THE ROXY ROLLER RINK Feb. 9, 1984

"CABLE HEALTH NETWORK" with Regis Philbin and
                        Cyndy Garvey March 5, 1984

KENNEDY CENTER HONORS JIMMY STEWART, KATHERINE DURHAM,
                        FRANK SINATRA CBS Dec. 27, 1983

PONY SNEAKERS (TV Commercial currently being aired)

FRENCH-ANTILLES TOUR: GUADELOUPE,MARTINIQUE,GUYANE. MAY 15-JUNE 5, 1984.

     TORINO, ITALY "DANCE FESTIVAL" JUNE 18-22, 1984.

     "THE MORNING SHOW" with REGIS PHILBIN ABC-TV JUNE 27,1984.
CLUBS:

     N.Y.C.: THE ROXY, THE RITZ, THE RED PARROT, DANCETERIA,

              and STUDIO 54.

     L.I. : REDS, KISS

     QUEENS: ECLIPSE, U.S.A. ROLLER RINK

     TORONTO, CANADA: THE TWILIGHT ZONE

     MONTREAL, CANADA: CLUB SODA March 23, 1984

     They have also appeared at major clubs in Boston, Washington, D.C.,

     New Jersey, Texas and Chicago.

There were more pages, but this is the only one I still have.

Cast ⌐ ¹l Sheet ~~for Beat Street~~
~~V.OC~~

Date: Monday, July 16th

Time	Location	Group
7:00 AM	Paul's Coffee Shcp SW Corner 89th/B'way	Sam, Clown and L'il Shake Alice Cox
8:00 AM	212 W. 105th St. (B'way/Amsterdam)	Robert Taylor Dynamic Dolls
9:30 AM	212 W.105th St. (B'way/Amsterdam)	Dynamic Breakers
12:00 Noon	Monument 89th/Riverside	Disc Dancers Annette Popatron Freedom Breakers High Performance Dynamic Juniors Rockwell Breakers Slow Motion
4:00 PM	Monument 89th/Riverside	Kids At Work 2nd St. Breakers Non-StopBreakers High Performance: Oli Carlos Davido All Star Breakers Jamaica Breakers Baby Dynamics Fresh Force All other extras

Note: Call Laurita Roc at 496-6762 with any questions.

Remember: If you aren't on time, the shooting will happen without
you!

Left: Legendary Shabba Doo and Kim-A-Kazi having breakfast in Las Vegas

Right: Kano (R) with his son Tim (L) after visiting us in Las Vegas @ The Grand Canyon

Left:The entrance to The Fun House

Right:Jose & Mickey, members of The Juice Crew

Now this is old school – handmade poster, no computer images!
Fresh

3D stickers of The Dynamic Dolls

Sylvia Browne and Kim-A-Kazi in Las Vegas

Jamie Foxx used to pass by my job and say hi to me whenever he was in Caesars Palace. I also became friends with iconic director George Sidney and his lovely wife, Corrine; they used to come see me every week after they dined at The Palms, where their famous characters were drawn over the doorway inside the restaurant. They invited me to their home, but unfortunately, I never got the chance to visit before George passed on.

Idalis DeLeon, a Juice Crew member, outside The Fun House. It just got raided.

216

Idalis later became a V.J. on MTV and appeared on the last few episodes of "Living Single" starring Queen Latifah.

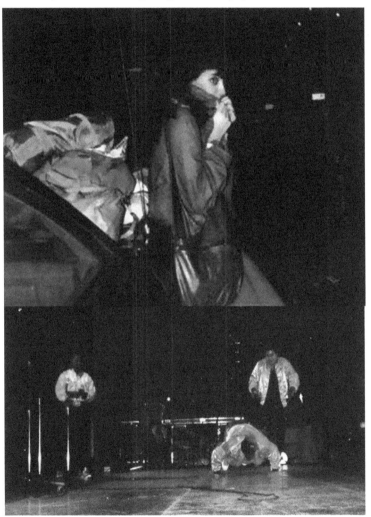

The Fat Boys – Buffy doing the worm!

Original photo during the photo shoot we did for The Muppet Magazine, where we appeared in the centerfold. I stood in the back because I wanted to be near my favorite Muppet, Animal. On the following page you can see the same photo as it appeared in The Muppet Magazine.

On the following page: These were two separate pages. I did my best to line them up. There are a few more pages with our interview, and a few pictures— I am sure you get the idea. This was a lot of fun and an honor working with Jim Henson.

Mother and Son (sun)

Kim-A-Kazi, Mom, Kristine (sister) / Kim-A-Kazi in Mexico

Mom and Dad / My uncle who got me interested in gymnastics

He is 70! Not bad, huh?

Kim-A-Kazi & JaeCie / Our last visit to the Fun House

Mr. Speed, Kim-A-Kazi, Eddie (Furious Rockers) / Dynamic Dolls

Buffy (The Fat Boys) signing autographs

Laurita (manager) and The Dynamic Breakers/Dolls off to Great Adventures for a show

B-Girls

They have come a long way since the 1980s, and I couldn't be happier or more proud. Today's B-Girls are now born into a world where Hip Hop is an established and flourishing culture, which just may become an Olympic event! You say "Nay"?

I say, "We shall see."

Each generation has to improve, has to take it to the next level and create moves that we who came before them couldn't even have imagined. I feel that is happening.

From myself, Kim-A-Kazi and The Dynamic Dolls, to the next generation, such as Ana "Rokafella" Garcia and B-Girl Veester, the torch has been passed. I know that each generation will set the bar higher, because to become a B-Girl, especially one of the best, you have to be made of something great. You must have passion, talent, and the conviction that females can do anything males can do— and the guts to get out there and prove it. We have earned the right to stand side by side with B-Boys, with many B-Girls earning respect by winning battles against them as well.

Yes, The Dynamic Dolls were the first, but there have been many B-Girls who have come along since, like Ana "Rokafella" Garcia (isn't that a great name?). Ana, along with her husband Gabriel "Kwikstep" Dionisio, have become mentors as well as Hip Hop dance instructors. They host all kinds of events— a great pair.

There has yet to be a documentary or a televised show on the real B-Girls. They have done shows about women in Hip Hop, but they mostly have women in the music categories, like Queen Latifah and Salt-N-Pepa. They definitely deserve recognition, but what about the B-Girls? Most people don't even know about The Dynamic Dolls, and those who do know about us do not offer up our history.

I would love it if somebody in the business who is without prejudice and who appreciates real Hip Hop history put our story out there. I have spoken about how it drives me crazy that when these big break dancing, Hip Hop movies come out, the B-Boys rule the screen and the females they use in these movies are more like backup dancers. Why don't they use real B-Girls? YouTube is filled with amazingly skilled B-Girls— why aren't they using them up on the big screen?

B-Girls are not going away. They are here to stay, and with each new generation they will get even more amazing. I hope to see equality for B-Girls while I am still here.

B-Girl – Kim-A-Kazi

B-Girl – Rokafella; photo by Yu Wadee

B-Girl – Veester

Shout Outs

Darlene Lewis– Brenda K. Starr— JaeCie Cruz— Dynamic Rockers— Incredible Breakers– Kurtis Blow– Keith Rodgers– Frosty Freeze (RIP)– The Fat Boys– Charles Stettler–Whodini –UTFO– Run DMC— Jam Master J– Tony Tone & The Cold Crush Brothers –Grand Master Caz— Uncle Monk, "The Fun House" Celestino — Nicholas Abreu— The Original Body Mechanix— Peter Rios III— Donald D. Bronx— TG Gaines— Elio "Spinner" Perez– Michael Holman–Michele Hairston— Jimmy Spicer— Jesse Manriquez— BBLT– Blackman Tfrc– Samantha Allende— Michael "Boogaloo Shrimp" Chambers – Romeo King— JT Thompson— Shabba-Doo— Manu Waa— Rodney Elkins— David Perelez— Mom— Louis Valente— Barry Tillery— Joe A Cooley— DJ Mike Scott— Suga Pop— Nelson Cruz— Float – Tony "Mr. Wave— Jaz Ford— Dune Uno— Jerri Council— Chris "Shake" Mathis— George Lumpkins— Darnez Levy— Ralph "Kinguprock" Casanova— Nika Kramer— Frank Vega— Robert Taylor (better known as "Lee" from the movie "Break Street")— Richard "Fast Break" Williams– Ana "Rokafella" Garcia– Gabriel "Kwikstep" Dionisio – The Roxy – The Fun House Laurita Rock– Cord Hamilton, Breakdance International.

And of course, The Dynamic Dolls and The Dynamic Breakers— and a special shoutout to all the B-Girls & B-Boys old school, new school, and everyone in between. To all the DJs, MCs, rappers, writers, producers, graffiti artists, and all who helped shape the Hip Hop culture, I salute you.

Peace and Blessings,

Kim *"Kim-A-Kazi"* Valente

Old School Graduates"

Back in the day, we didn't have any teachers,

We taught ourselves every skill that we featured.

Rappin, scratchin, break dancing & Pop,

Taggin', graffiti, we all created Hip Hop.

The moves, styles and the beats were our creations

We faced and we battled all kinds of discriminations.

We laid the foundation and we created a path

for future generations, though some said it wouldn't last.

Now Hip Hop is a culture, a **Way of Life,**

All our blood, sweat and tears were worth the fight.

So all you young'uns and up-comin's it is now your turn to shine,

But on your way up don't forget to look **behind**, and pay tribute to

The *Graduates* from the *Old School.* We pushed and we struggled, we broke every rule,

We raised our voices until we made them hear,

We refused to be *ignored;* our message was clear.

So pay tribute to the **Old School,** for we paved the way

And made sure that **Hip Hop** was here to stay,

We came a very long way, without all of the opportunities that you now have today.

Written by: Kim-A-Kazi–2010

Please look for other books written by Kim L. Valente

The Secret She Hid in the Night; 2011

A B-Girl in a B-Boy World; 2015

Look for these titles and others to come at:

Yahoo.com

Amazon.com

Barnes & Noble

And other major online bookstores.

About the Author

Born and raised in Brooklyn, New York, Kim now resides in Las Vegas, Nevada, with her husband and her son. Dancing and writing are her two greatest passions.

Currently, Kim is working on her next two books. *The Last Straw* is a riveting page-turner and *Beware the Devil's Charm* is a dark, sinister story from the inner thoughts of a psychopathic murderer.

Kim writes in all genres and is eager to publish her children's stories as well. She would like to use her gift of connecting with children to lecture at schools around the country.

"I want to share with children many of the things I wish someone would have passed on to me," Kim says. "I want all children to know they can be whatever they want no matter where they came from. And in me, I think they can see for themselves that is possible."

As for the adults, she says to never give up on your dreams.

"It took me fifty years, but I am finally writing."

Milton Keynes UK
Ingram Content Group UK Ltd.
UKHW051702070424
440754UK00009B/110